UNJUSTIFIABLY OPPRESSED

Black Codes of Mississippi (1865)

UNJUSTIFIABLY OPPRESSED

Black Codes of Mississippi (1865)

◆

Roderick Van Daniel, Ph. D. & J.D.

Van Daniel Marketing, LLC
Aberdeen Birmingham DC Memphis Atlanta Boston

UNJUSTIFIABLY OPPRESSED

Van Daniel Marketing, LLC

For information address:
Van Daniel Marketing, LLC
roddaniel205@gmail.com
(662) 304 - 0896

Printed in the United States of America

"Freedom has never been free."

> — Medgar Evers

"As a nation, we began by declaring that 'all men are created equal'. We now practically read it 'all men are created equal, except negroes'. When the Know-Nothings get control, it will read 'all men are created equal, except negroes, foreigners, and Catholics'."

> — Abraham Lincoln (August 24, 1855)

"Let's tell the truth if it bursts the bottom of the Universe...We came here to exclude the Negro. Nothing short of this will answer."

> — Solomon Saladin Calhoon (Mississippi Constitutional Convention of 1890)

Contents

Dedicated to my mother,
Yvonne Daniel

Acknowledgement

◆

This book is dedicated to my mother, Yvonne Daniel, for listening to my dreams, encouraging me to achieve my goals, and providing the support for me to be strong. Mom, you have inspired me from the moment you gave birth to me. I love you. You instilled in me the importance of education but more importantly to graduate with the degree. Thanks for always encouraging me to keep the Lord with me on my educational journey and in my everyday life. Mom, thank you for the financial support. I never would have made it without you. I love you so much.

This book is also dedicated to my brothers, Dashmond and Zerdock, sister, Ashalond Daniel, and my father Roy Garth. You gave me strength each day. Thank you for believing that dreams do come true; I did it!

To my grandmother, Clara Betts Daniel, thank you for instilling the Lord in my life. I miss you. Thank you for telling me that I have to be strong to survive in this world. Thank you for telling me to hold my head up high and not walk with it down. Thank you for making me come inside the house before the street lights came on at night. I want to thank you for loving me and telling me that you have to leave the nest sometimes to truly become the man that you desire to become. Thank you for telling me to carry the Lord's scripture in my pocket every day, "The Lord is my shepard; I shall not want." I thank you for being strong; you made me strong through being around you. You lived to be in your nineties; you gave me wisdom and strength beyond my childhood years. I miss you. I love you still.

Only the strong survive, you told me to remember that always. I stand strong for you and my family. I thank you.

To Dr. Prince, Coach Roy Hazzle, and Coach Ball-Williamson; I also thank you for giving me an opportunity to learn from your wisdom. I value you all.

Thank you God and Jesus for I can do all things because you all strengthen me. Thanks for making me strong in your word and truth; I love you both as well.

Southern Past

"I grew up on the banks of the Tombigbee River in the town of Aberdeen, Mississippi. Aberdeen has a lot of history about slavery and the effects of the Black Codes of Mississippi established in1865 after the Civil War. The Black Codes of Mississippi has had a prolonged and lasting impact on the freedoms expressed in the Constitution of the United States of America for equality for all people in this country."

-Dr. Roderick Van Daniel

President James Monroe on December 10, 1817 signed the resolution that admitted Mississippi as the nation's 20th state. The people were concentrated in two principal areas in Mississippi – the Natchez District and the lower Tombigbee settlements above and west of Mobile. Approximately 4,500 people, including slaves, lived at Natchez, considerably more than the combined free and slave population of 1,250 that inhabited the Tombigbee settlements in 1800. Outside of these two areas, the territory was populated only by American Indians. The state of Mississippi became "The King of Cotton" from the harsh labor of Negro slaves from Africa. In 1860, the single wealthiest county per capita in the United States was Adams County, Mississippi. As the Confederate States of America, the South by itself was the 4th wealthiest nation in the world. Eighty-five percent of the cotton Southern slaves picked were shipped to Britain.

HOLLIDAY PLACE PLANTATION - 1850

The slaves often rebelled from the cruelty subjected to them by their white slave masters and the overseers which included cutting off body parts, whipping with lashes all over the body but mainly the back, and torture.

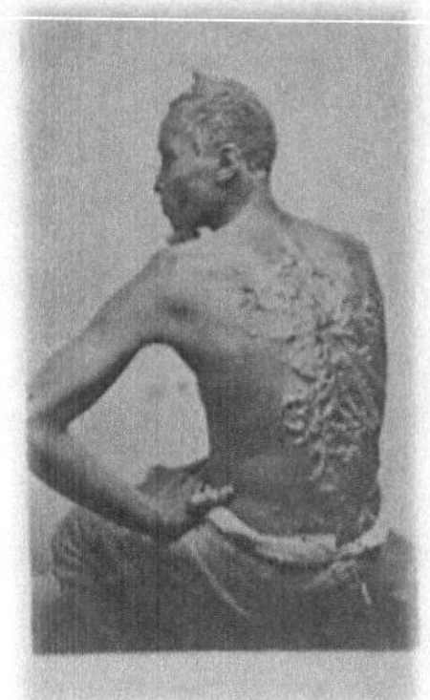

The desire for freedom, and the need to escape inhumane treatment, was the motives for slaves to rebel against their white slave masters. Agricultural was the center of the South and cotton was the center of prosperity for white plantation owners by using Negroes (African Americans) as slaves. Mississippi was one of the first states to secede first from the Union and the last to return. Mississippians reasoning for not wanting to emancipate the slaves were all related to money, power, and the economics of cotton for the state on an international market. They had enslaved their workforce for generations. The state of Mississippi population was 55 percent Negroes (African Americans) before the Civil War.

The American Civil War was fought between 1861 to 1865. Among the 34 U.S. states in February 1861, seven Southern states individually declared secession from the country to form the Confederate States of America. The Confederacy grew to include eleven states, all of them slaveholding: Alabama, Arizona, Arkansas, Florida, Georgia, Louisiana, Mississippi, New Mexico, North Carolina, South Carolina, Tennessee, Texas, and Virginia.

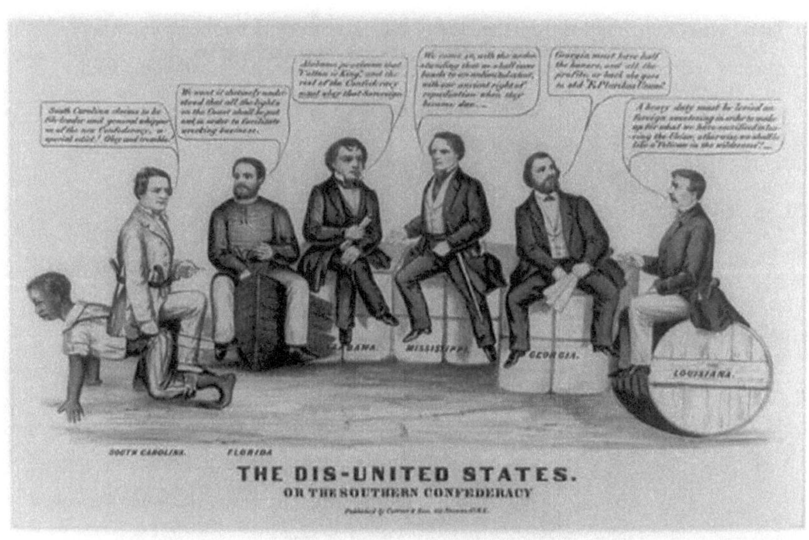
SOUTH CAROLINA.
FLORIDA
ALABAMA.
MISSISSIPPI.
GEORGIA.
LOUISIANA.
THE DIS-UNITED STATES.
OR THE SOUTHERN CONFEDERACY

In the wake of the Civil War, some four millions slaves were freed by the Emancipation Proclamation and the Union victory. However, the South had been severely damaged by war, leaving communities and the economy in ruin. To provide aid in the form of food, housing, medical care, and education for former slaves and poor whites, the Freedman's Bureau was established by Congress in 1865.

Five days after the Civil War ended, President Abraham Lincoln was shot. He died on April 15, 1865, and Vice President Andrew Johnson assumed the presidency. With the Freedman's Bureau establishment came hope, which was quickly pushed back against by mainly southern whites and President Andrew Johnson. Johnson fought with Congress and the Reconstruction policies, removing anyone from the Freedman's Bureau that was "too sympathetic" to blacks and granting pardons to many former Confederates, restoring them of their land. He worked to undermine the authority of the Freedman's Bureau, contributing it its difficulties and failings. President Andrew Johnson was born a southerner. At this time, the free slaves had the right to vote.

In Mississippi Colonel Samuel Thomas, the assistant commissioner of the Freedmen's Bureau who opened the Bureau office in Vicksburg, noticed white Mississippians' defiant posture when he traveled through the state months after the Civil War.

"Wherever I go—the street, the shop, the house, or the steamboat—I hear the people talk in such a way as to indicate that they are yet unable to conceive of the Negro as possessing any rights at all." Thomas worried that whites "who are honorable in their dealings with their white neighbors will cheat a Negro without feeling a single twinge of their honor. To kill a Negro they do not deem murder." Such men openly boasted to Thomas that blacks "will catch hell" when local whites re-acquired political control. Trying to explain this defiance, Thomas pointed to prejudices seared into white minds and hearts during the era of slavery. As Thomas put it, though white Mississippians "admit that the individual relations of masters and slaves have been destroyed by the war and the President's emancipation proclamation, they still have an ingrained feeling that the blacks at large belong to the whites at large."

The Mississippi Black Codes of 1865 triggered a storm of protest among many Northerners. They accused Southern whites of trying to reestablish slavery by using these black codes. These codes were the replacement for the slave codes but for free slaves with similar harsh treatments to the negroes (African American). The Southern whites did not want to treat the free slaves fairly under the law of the state.

Along with the Black Codes, other events helped alter the course of Reconstruction: The 14th Amendment passed, and a new Congress hostile to the South was elected. This Congress took control of Reconstruction. When President Johnson vetoed Congress Reconstruction legislation, Congress overrode his vetoes. The battles with Johnson led ultimately in 1868 to his impeachment by the House, the first impeachment of a president in American history. (The Senate failed to convict him by one vote.)

Under the direction of Congress, most Southern states held new constitutional conventions in 1867–68. This time the free slaves voted and participated. The resulting new state constitutions guaranteed the right of black adult males to vote and run for political (public) office. For the first time, some blacks won election to Southern state legislatures and to Congress. By 1868, most states had repealed the remains of discriminatory Black Code laws.

But Reconstruction did not last as long as it should have. By 1877, it was dead for trying to help the free slaves be a part of a country that enslaved them for hundreds of years. The North had lost interest in helping Southern blacks. Many factors helped kill Reconstruction from economic troubles in the country, a more conservative consensus within the nation, a general feeling in the country that Reconstruction had failed, the resurgence of the white supremacist political party, and a growing respectability for racist attitudes.

Southern states such as Mississippi began trying to end voting for African Americans (ex-slaves). By 1910, all Southern states had excluded blacks from voting. In the 1890s, Southern states enacted a new form of Black Codes, called "Jim Crow" laws. These laws made it illegal for blacks and whites to share public facilities. This meant that blacks and whites had to use separate schools, hospitals, libraries, restaurants, hotels, bathrooms, and drinking fountains. These laws stayed in effect until the 1950s and 1960s, when the civil rights movement launched an all-out campaign against them.

"Southern Past"

Black Codes of Mississippi

Black Codes of Mississippi

"Let's tell the truth if it bursts the bottom of the Universe...We came here to exclude the Negro. Nothing short of this will answer."

- *Solomon Saladin Calhoon (Mississippi Constitutional Convention of 1890)*

On November 24, 1865, the Black Codes of Mississippi were passed. Mississippi was the first state to pass such laws, and, eventually all Southern states would pass similar laws. The status of the Negro was the fundamental problem of Reconstruction. Slavery had been abolished by the Thirteenth Amendment, but the white people of the South including Mississippi were determined to keep the Negro in his place, socially, politically, and economically. Mississippi had the harshest body of statutes for the "Black Codes". Four of the statutes that made up the code will be listed below. Try to

understand the laws and the continued oppression that the slaves but
now freedmen and women had to endure to try to be free striving for equality in a
country that always wanted Negroes (African Americans) to always be in service
 to the whites in America and across the world.

*"As a nation, we began by declaring that 'all men are created equal'.
We now practically read it 'all men are created equal, except negroes'.
When the Know-Nothings get control, it will read 'all men are created
equal, except negroes, foreigners, and Catholics'."*

 – Abraham Lincoln (August 24, 1855)

Black Codes of Mississippi (1865)

Apprentice Law

Section 1. *Be it enacted by the legislature of the state of Mississippi,* that it shall be the duty of all sheriffs, justices of the peace, and other civil officers of the several counties in this state to report to the Probate courts of their respective counties semiannually, at the January and July terms of said courts, all freedmen, free Negroes, and mulattoes under the age of eighteen within their respective counties, beats, or districts who are orphans, or whose parent or parents have not the means, or who refuse to provide for and support said minors; and thereupon it shall be the duty of said Probate Court to order the clerk of said court to apprentice said minors to some competent and suitable person, on such terms as the court may direct, having a particular care to the interest of said minors:

Provided, that the former owner of said minors shall have the preference when, in the opinion of the court, he or she shall be a Suitable person for that purpose.

Section 2. *Be it further enacted,* that the said court shall be fully satisfied that the person or persons to whom said minor shall be apprenticed shall be a suitable person to have the charge and care of said minor and fully to protect the interest of said minor. The said court shall require the said master or mistress to execute bond and security, payable to the state of Mississippi, conditioned that he or she shall furnish said minor with sufficient food and clothing; to treat said minor humanely; furnish medical attention in case of sickness; teach or cause to be taught him or her to read and write, if under fifteen years old; and will conform to any law that may be hereafter passed for the regulation of the duties and relation of master and apprentice:

Provided, that said apprentice shall be bound by indenture, in case of males until they are twenty-one years old, and in case of females until they are eighteen years old.

Section 3. *Be it further enacted,* that in the management and control of said apprentices, said master or mistress shall have power to inflict such moderate corporeal chastisement as a father or guardian is allowed to inflict on his or her child or ward at common law:

Provided, that in no case shall cruel or inhuman punishment be inflicted.

Section 4. *Be it further enacted,* that if any apprentice shall leave the employment of his or her master or mistress without his or her consent, said master or mistress may pursue and recapture said apprentice and bring him or her before any justice of the peace of the county, whose duty it shall be to remand said apprentice to the service of his or her master or mistress; and in the event of a refusal on the part of said apprentice so to return, then said justice shall commit said apprentice to the jail of said county, on failure to give bond, until the next term of the county court; and it shall be the duty of said court, at the first term thereafter, to investigate said case; and if the court shall be of opinion that said apprentice left the employment of his or her master or mistress without good cause, to order him or her to be punished, as provided for the punishment of hired freedmen, as may be from time to time provided for by law, for desertion, until he or she shall agree to return to his or her master or mistress:

Provided, that the court may grant continuances, as in other cases; and *provided,* further, that if the court shall believe that said apprentice had good cause to quit his said master or mistress, the court shall discharge said apprentice from said indenture and also enter a judgment against the master or mistress for not more than $100, for the use and benefit of said apprentice, to be collected on execution, as in other cases.

Section 5. *Be it further enacted,* that if any person entice away any apprentice from his or her master or mistress, or shall knowingly employ an apprentice, or furnish him or her food or clothing, without the written consent of his or her master or mistress, of shall sell or give said apprentice ardent spirits, without such consent, said person so offending shall be deemed guilty of a high misdemeanor, and shall, on conviction thereof before the county court, be punished as provided for the punishment of persons enticing from their employer hired freedmen, free Negroes, or mulattoes.

Section 6. *Be it further enacted,* that it shall be the duty of all civil officers of their respective counties to report any minors within their respective counties to said Probate Court who are subject to be apprenticed under the provisions of this act, from time to time, as the facts may come to their knowledge; and it shall be the duty of said court, from time to time, as said minors shall be reported to them or otherwise come to their knowledge, to apprentice said minors as hereinbefore provided.

Section 7. *Be it further enacted,* that in case the master or mistress of any apprentice shall desire, he or she shall have the privilege to summon his or her said apprentice to the Probate Court, and thereupon, with the approval of the court, he or she shall be released from all liability as master of said apprentice, and his said bond shall be canceled, and it shall be the duty of the court forthwith to reapprentice said minor; and in the event any master of in apprentice shall die before the close of the term of service of said apprentice, it shall be the duty of the court to give the preference in reapprenticing said minor to the widow, or other member of said master's family:

Provided, that said widow or other member of said family shall be a suitable person for that purpose.

Section 8. *Be it further enacted,* that in case any master or mistress of any apprentice, bound to him or her under this act shall be about to remove or shall have removed to any other state of the United States by the laws of which such apprentice may be an inhabitant thereof, the Probate Court of the proper county may authorize the removal of such apprentice to such state, upon the said master or mistress entering into bond, with security, in a penalty to be fixed by the judge, conditioned that said master or mistress will, upon such removal, comply with the laws of such state in such cases:

Provided, that said master shall be cited to attend the court at which such order is proposed to be made and shall have a right to resist the same by next friend, or otherwise.

Section *9. Be it further enacted,* that it shall be lawful for any freedman, free Negro, or Mulatto having a minor child or children to apprentice the said minor child or children as provided for by this act.

Section 10. *Be it further enacted,* that in all cases where the age of the freedman, free Negro, or mulatto cannot be ascertained by record testimony, the judge of the county court shall fix the age.

II.

Vagrancy Law

Section 1. *Be it enacted by the legislature of the state of Mississippi,* that all rogues and vagabonds, idle and dissipated persons, beggars, jugglers, or persons practising unlawful games or plays, runaways, common drunkards, common nightwalkers, pilferers, lewd, wanton, or lascivious persons, in speech or behavior, common railers and brawlers, persons who neglect their calling or employment, misspend what they earn, or do not provide for the support of themselves or their families or dependents, and all other idle and disorderly persons, including all who neglect all lawful business, or habitually misspend their time by frequenting houses of ill-fame, gaming houses, or tippling shops, shall be deemed and considered vagrants under the provisions of this act; and, on conviction thereof shall be fined not exceeding $100, with all accruing costs, and be imprisoned at the discretion of the court not exceeding ten days.

Section *2. Be it further enacted,* that all freedmen, free Negroes, and mulattoes in this state over the age of eighteen years found on the second Monday in January 1966, or thereafter, with no lawful employment or business, or found unlawfully assembling themselves together either in the day or nighttime, and all white persons so assembling with freedmen, free Negroes, or mulattoes, or usually associating with freedmen, free Negroes, or mulattoes on terms of equality, or living in adultery or fornication with a freedwoman, free Negro, or mulatto, shall be deemed vagrants; and, on conviction thereof, shall be fined in the sum of not exceeding, in the case of a freedman, free Negro, or mulatto, 150, and a white man, $200, and imprisoned at the discretion of the court, the free Negro not exceeding ten days, and the white man not exceeding six months.

Section 3. *Be it further enacted,* that all justices of the peace, mayors, and aldermen of incorporated towns and cities of the several counties in this state shall have jurisdiction to try all questions of vagrancy in their respective towns, counties, and cities; and it is hereby made their duty, whenever they shall ascertain that any person or persons in their respective towns, counties, and cities are violating any of the provisions of this act, to have said party or parties arrested and brought before them and immediately investigate said charge; and, on conviction, punish said party or parties as provided for herein. And it is hereby made the duty of all sheriffs, constables, town constables, city marshals, and all like officers to report to some officer having jurisdiction all violations of any of the provisions of this act; and it shall be the duty of the county courts to inquire if any officers have neglected any of the duties required by this act; and in case any officer shall fail or neglect any duty herein, it shall be the duty of the county court to fine said officer, upon conviction, not exceeding $100, to be paid into the county treasury for county purposes.

Section 4. *Be it further enacted,* that keepers of gaming houses, houses of prostitution, all prostitutes, public or private, and all persons who derive their chief support in employments that militate against good morals or against laws shall be deemed and held to be vagrants.

Section 5. *Be it further enacted,* that all fines and forfeitures collected under the provisions of this act shall be paid into the county treasury for general county purposes; and in case any freedman, free Negro, or mulatto shall fail for five days after the imposition of any fine or forfeiture upon him or her for violation of any of the provisions of this act to pay the same, that it shall be, and is hereby made, the duty of the sheriff of the proper county to hire out said freedman, free Negro, or mulatto to any person who will, for the shortest period of service, pay said fine or forfeiture and all costs:

Provided, a preference shall be given to the employer, if there be one, in which case the employer shall be entitled to deduct and retain the amount so paid from the wages of such freedman, free Negro, or mulatto then due or to become due; and in case such freedman, free Negro, or mulatto cannot be hired out he or she may be dealt with as a pauper.

Section 6. *Be it further enacted,* that the same duties and liabilities existing among white persons of this state shall attach to freedmen, free Negroes, and mulattoes to support their indigent families and all colored paupers; and that, in order to secure a support for such indigent freedmen, free Negroes, and mulattoes, it shall be lawful, and it is hereby made the duty of the boards of county police of each county in this state, to levy a poll or capitation tax on each and every freedman, free Negro, or mulatto, between the ages of eighteen and sixty years, not to exceed the sum of s I annually, to each person so taxed, which tax, when collected, shall be paid into the county treasurer's hands and constitute a fund to be called the Freedman's Pauper Fund, which shall be applied by the commissioners of the poor for the maintenance of the poor of the freedmen, free Negroes. and mulattoes of this state, under such regulations as may be established by the boards of county police, in the respective counties of this state.

Section 7. *Be it further enacted,* that if any freedman, free Negro, or mulatto shall fail or refuse to pay any tax levied according to the provisions of the 6th Section of this act, it shall be prima facie evidence of vagrancy, and it shall be the duty of the sheriff to arrest such freedman, free Negro, or mulatto, or such person refusing or neglecting to pay such tax, and proceed at once to hire, for the shortest time, such delinquent taxpayer to anyone who will pay the said tax, with accruing costs, giving preference to the employer, if there be one.

Section 8. *Be it further enacted,* that any person feeling himself or herself aggrieved by the judgment of any justice of the peace, mayor, or alderman in cases arising under this act may, within five days, appeal to the next term of the county court of the proper county, upon giving bond and security in a sum not less than $25 nor more than $150, conditioned to appear and prosecute said appeal, and abide by the judgment of the county court, and said appeal shall be tried *de novo* in the county court, and the decision of said court shall be final.

Civil Rights of Freedmen

Section 1. *Be it enacted by the legislature of the state of Mississippi,* that all freedmen, free Negroes, and mulattoes may sue and be sued, implead and be impleaded in all the courts of law and equity of this state, and may acquire personal property and choses in action, by descent or purchase, and may dispose of the same in the same manner and to the same extent that white persons may:

Provided, that the provisions of this section shall not be construed as to allow any freedman, free Negro, or mulatto to rent or lease any lands or tenements, except in incorporated towns or cities, in which places the corporate authorities shall control the same.

Section 2. *Be it further enacted,* that all freedmen, free Negroes, and mulattoes may intermarry with each other, in the same manner and under the same regulations that are provided by law for white persons:

Provided, that the clerk of probate shall keep separate records of the same.

Section 3. *Be it further enacted,* that all freedmen, free Negroes, and mulattoes who do now and have heretofore lived and cohabited together as husband and wife shall be taken and held in law as legally married, and the issue shall be taken and held as legitimate for all purposes. That it shall not be lawful for any freedman, free Negro, or mulatto to intermarry with any white person; nor for any white person to intermarry with any freedman, free Negro, or mulatto; and any person who shall so intermarry shall be deemed guilty of felony and, on conviction thereof, shall be confined in the state penitentiary for life; and those shall be deemed freedmen, free Negroes, and mulattoes who are of pure Negro blood; and those descended from a Negro to the third generation inclusive, though one ancestor of each generation may have been a white person.

Section 4. *Be it further enacted,* that in addition to cases in which freedmen, free Negroes, and mulattoes are now by law competent witnesses, freedmen, free Negroes, or mulattoes shall be competent in civil cases when a party or parties to the suit, either plaintiff or plaintiffs, defendant or defendants, also in cases where freedmen, free Negroes, and mulattoes is or are either plaintiff or plaintiffs, defendant or defendants, and a white person or white persons is or are the opposing party or parties, plaintiff or plaintiffs, defendant or defendants. They shall also be competent witnesses in all criminal prosecutions where the crime charged is alleged to have been committed by a white person upon or against the person or property of a freedman, free Negro, or mulatto:

Provided, that in all cases said witnesses shall be examined in open court on the stand, except, however, they may be examined before the grand jury, and shall in all cases be subject to the rules and tests of the common law as to competency and credibility.

Section 5. *Be it further enacted,* that every freedman, free Negro, and mulatto shall, on the second Monday of January 1866, and annually thereafter, have a lawful home or employment, and shall have a written evidence thereof, as follows, to wit: if living in any incorporated city, town, or village, a license from the mayor thereof; and if living outside of any incorporated city, town, or village, from the member of the board of police of his beat, authorizing him or her to do irregular and job work, or a written contract, as provided in Section 6 of this act, which licenses may be revoked for cause, at any time, by the authority granting the same.

Section 6. *Be it further enacted,* that all contracts for labor made with freedmen, free Negroes, and mulattoes for a longer period than one month shall be in writing and in duplicate, attested and read to said freedman, free Negro, or mulatto by a beat, city, or county officer, or two disinterested white persons of the county in which the labor is to be performed, of which each party shall have one; and said contracts shall be taken and held as entire contracts; and if the laborer shall quit the service of the employer before expiration of his term of service without good cause, he shall forfeit his wages for that year, up to the time of quitting.

Section 7. *Be it further enacted,* that every civil officer shall, and every person may, arrest and carry back to his or her legal employer any freedman, free Negro, or mulatto who shall have quit the service of his or her employer before the expiration of his or her term of service without good cause, and said officer and person shall be entitled to receive for arresting and carrying back every deserting employee

aforesaid the sum of $5, and 10 cents per mile from the place of arrest
to the place of delivery, and the same shall be paid by the employer,
and held as a setoff for so much against the wages of said deserting
employee:

Provided, that said arrested party, after being so returned, may appeal
to a justice of the peace or member of the board of police of the county,
who, on notice to the alleged employer, shall try summarily whether
said appellant is legally employed by the alleged employer and his
good cause to quit said employer; either party shall have the right of
appeal to the county court, pending which the alleged deserter shall be
remanded to the alleged employer or otherwise disposed of as shall be
right and just, and the decision of the county court shall be final.

Section 8. *Be it further enacted,* that upon affidavit made by the
employer of any freedman, free Negro, or mulatto, or other credible
person before any justice of the peace or member of the board of
police, that any freedman, free Negro, or mulatto, legally employed by
said employer, has illegally deserted said employment, such justice of
the peace or member of the board of police shall issue his warrant or
warrants, returnable before himself, or other such officer, directed to
any sheriff, constable, or special deputy, commanding him to arrest
said deserter and return him or her to said employer, and the like
proceedings shall be had as provided in the preceding section; and it
shall be lawful for any officer to whom such warrant shall be directed
to execute said warrant in any county of this state, and that said warrant
may be transmitted without endorsement to any like officer of another
county, to be executed and returned as aforesaid, and the said employer
shall pay the cost of said warrants and arrest and return, which shall be
set off for so much against the wages of said deserter.

Section *9. Be it further enacted,* that if any person shall persuade or attempt to persuade, entice, or cause any freedman, free Negro, or mulatto to desert from the legal employment of any person before the expiration of his or her term of service, or shall knowingly employ any such deserting freedman, free Negro, or mulatto, or shall knowingly give or sell to any such deserting freedman, free Negro, or mulatto any food, raiment, or other thing, he or she shall be guilty of a misdemeanor; and, upon conviction, shall be fined not less than $25 and not more than $200 and the costs; and, if said fine and costs shall not be immediately paid, the court shall sentence said convict to not exceeding two months' imprisonment in the county jail, and he or she shall moreover be liable to the party injured in damages:

Provided, if any person shall, or shall attempt to, persuade, entice, or cause any freedman, free Negro, or mulatto to desert from any legal employment of any person with the view to employ said freedman, free Negro, or mulatto without the limits of this state, such person, on conviction, shall be fined not less than $50 and not more than $1500 and costs; and, if said fine and costs shall not be immediately paid, the court shall sentence said convict to not exceeding six months' imprisonment in the county jail,

Section 10. *Be it further enacted,* that it shall be lawful for any freedman, free Negro, or mulatto to charge any white person, freedman, free Negro, or mulatto, by affidavit, with any criminal offense against his or her person or property; and, upon such affidavit, the proper process shall be issued and executed as if said affidavit was made by a white person; and it shall be lawful for any freedman, free Negro, or mulatto, in any action, suit, or controversy pending or about to be instituted, in any court of law or equity of this state. to make all needful and lawful affidavits, as shall be necessary for the institution, prosecution, or defense of such suit or controversy.

Section 11. *Be it further enacted,* that the penal laws of this state, in all cases not otherwise specially provided for, shall apply and extend to all freedmen, free Negroes, and mulattoes.

IV.

Penal Code

Section 1. *Be it enacted by the legislature of the state of Mississippi,* that no freedman, free Negro, or mulatto not in the military service of the United States government, and not licensed so to do by the board of police of his or her county, shall keep or carry firearms of any kind, or any ammunition, dirk, or Bowie knife; and, on conviction *thereof in the county* court, shall be punished by fine, not exceeding $10, and pay the costs of such proceedings, and all such arms or ammunition shall be forfeited to the informer; and it shall be the duty of every civil and military officer to arrest any freedman, free Negro, or mulatto found with any such arms or ammunition, and cause him or her to be committed for trial in default of bail.

Section 2. *Be it further enacted,* that any freedman, free Negro, or mulatto committing riots, routs, affrays, trespasses, malicious mischief, cruel treatment to animals, seditious speeches, insulting gestures, language, or acts, or assaults on any person, disturbance of the peace, exercising the function of a minister of the Gospel without a license from some regularly organized church, vending spirituous or intoxicating liquors, or committing any other misdemeanor t e punishment of which is not specifically provided for by law shall, upon conviction thereof in the county court, be fined not less than $10 and not more than $100, and may be imprisoned, at the discretion of the court, not exceeding thirty days.

Section 3. *Be it further enacted,* that if any white person shall sell, lend, or give to any freedman, free Negro, or mulatto any firearms, dirk, or Bowie knife, or ammunition, or any spirituous or intoxicating liquors, such person or persons so offending, upon conviction thereof

in the county court of his or her county, shall be fined not exceeding
$50, and may be imprisoned, at the discretion of the court, not
exceeding thirty days:

Provided, that any master, mistress, or employer of any freedman, free
Negro, or mulatto may give to any freedman, free Negro, or mulatto
apprenticed to or employed by such master, mistress, or employer
spirituous or intoxicating liquors, but not in sufficient quantities to
produce intoxication.

Section 4. *Be it further enacted,* that all the penal and criminal laws
now in force in this state defining offenses and prescribing the mode of
punishment for crimes and misdemeanors committed by slaves, free
Negroes, or mulattoes be and the same are hereby reenacted and
declared to be in full force and effect against freedmen, free Negroes,
and mulattoes, except so far m the mode and manner of trial and
punishment have been changed or altered by law.

Section 5. *Be it further enacted,* that if any freedman, free Negro, or
mulatto convicted of any of the misdemeanors provided against in this
act shall fail-or refuse, for the space of five days after conviction, to
pay the fine and costs imposed, such person shall be hired out by the
sheriff or other officer, at public outcry, to any white person who will
pay said fine and all costs and take such convict for the shortest time.
(Westport, Conn., 1972) Ark. Narr., Vol. 8, 175- 179.

"Black Codes of Mississippi"

Images of Mississippi

Images of Mississippi

"The Lord is the strength of my life; of whom shall I be afraid." Psalm 27:1

Vicksburg, Mississippi: Black Family living on Cotton Plantation

Vicksburg, Mississippi: Negroes Men at the Barbershop

Vicksburg, Mississippi: Negro Slave Quarters

Meridian, Mississippi: Negro Red Cross

Clarksdale, Mississippi: Negro' s Bar and Grill on Saturday

Mound Bayou, Mississippi: Talking in the street downtown

Belzoni, Mississippi: Negro going into movies through the back

Perthshire, Mississippi: Josh Taylor lived on the Knowlton
Plantation for 53 years

Scott, Mississippi: Negro going to the Delta and Pin Cotton Gin

Mileston, Mississippi: Negro tenant sitting on sack of cotton at the Marcella Plantation

Clarksdale, Mississippi: Negro Tenant farmers selling cotton

Mileston, Mississippi: Cotton on porch of Negro Tenant's home

Vicksburg, Mississippi: Negro Church on the Mississippi River

Aberdeen, Mississippi: Barbershop

Aberdeen, Mississippi: Local Negro man posing for picture

Aberdeen, Mississippi: Edmond Sims (1900) living in local area

Aberdeen, Mississippi: Cotton Gin on Commerce Street

Aberdeen, Mississippi: Downtown in 1890

Aberdeen, Mississippi: Negroes Library

Aberdeen, Mississippi: Horace Willis (1920) farmer

Aberdeen, Mississippi: Harriet (Steele) Whitley at their store
called Whitley' s grocery on corner of Burnette and Columbus
Street - Black ownership

Aberdeen, Mississippi: Mrs. Carrie Steele (1900) Negro woman

Aberdeen, Mississippi: Lenoir Plantation built in 1847

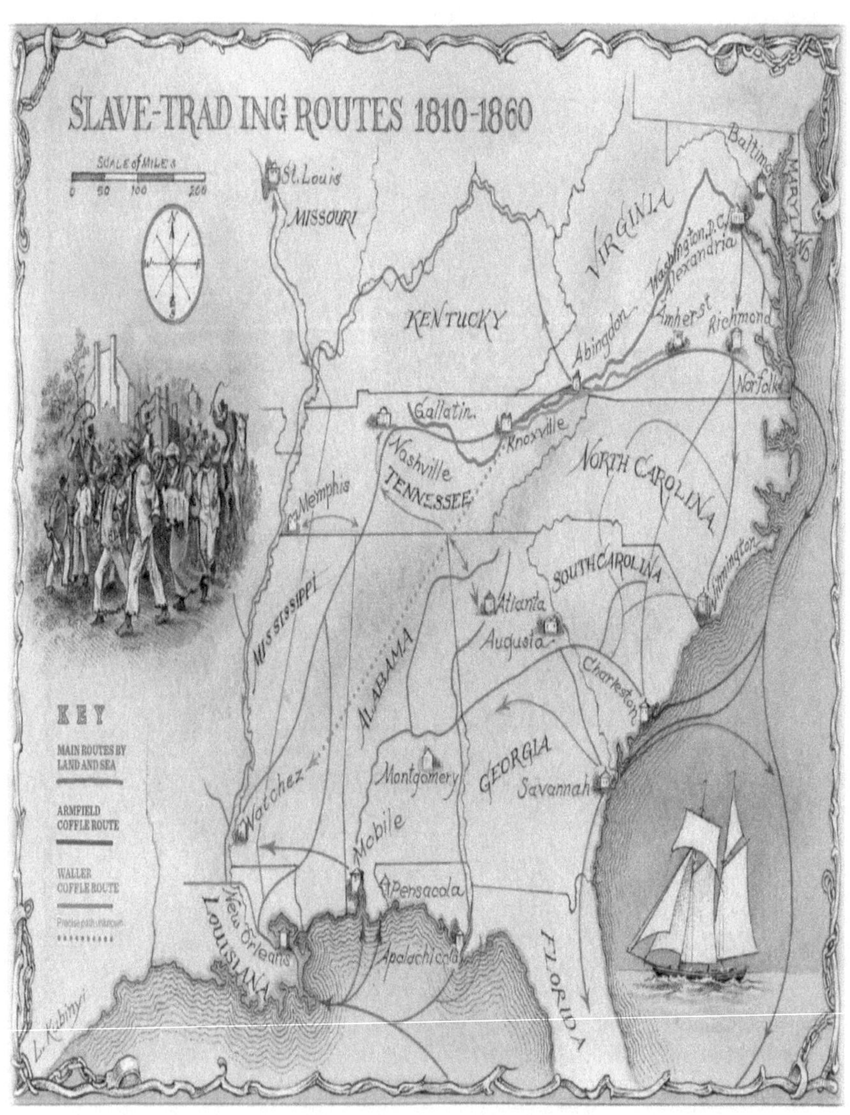

SLAVE-TRADING ROUTES 1810-1860
SCALE of MILES
0   50   100   200
St. Louis
MISSOURI
VIRGINIA
Baltimore
MARYLAND
Washington, D.C.
Alexandria
KENTUCKY
Abingdon
Amherst
Richmond
Gallatin
Knoxville
Norfolk
Nashville
NORTH CAROLINA
Memphis
TENNESSEE
Wilmington
SOUTH CAROLINA
Atlanta
Augusta
MISSISSIPPI
ALABAMA
Charleston
KEY
MAIN ROUTES BY
LAND AND SEA
ARMFIELD
COFFLE ROUTE
WALLER
COFFLE ROUTE
Precise path unknown
Natchez
Montgomery
GEORGIA
Savannah
Mobile
New Orleans
Pensacola
LOUISIANA
Apalachicola
FLORIDA
L. Kubinyi

Aberdeen, Mississippi: White men, an African-American man, and a child standing outside W. L. Watkins & Co.

Holmes County, Mississippi: Negro women picking cotton

SLAVES! SLAVES!! SLAVES!!!
FORKS OF THE ROAD, NATCHEZ.

THE SUBSCRIBERS have just arrived in Natchez, and are now stopping at Mr. Elam's house, Forks of the Road, with a choice selection of slaves, consisting of MECHANICS, FIELD HANDS, COOKS, WASHERS AND IRONERS, and GENERAL HOUSE SERVANTS.

They will be constantly receiving additions to their present supply during the season, and will be sold at as reasonable rates as can be afforded in this market.

To those purchasers desiring it, the Louisiana guarantee will be given.

Planters and others desirous of purchasing, are requested to call and see the Slaves before purchasing elsewhere.   nov27—d:wtf   GRIFFIN & PULLUM.

Mules!   Mules!   Mules!

JUST ARRIVED, and in excellent order. A large lot of MULES, raised in Missouri, and recommended for their size and condition.

They can be seen at the mule yards of Mr. Joseph E. Kirk, and will be sold on favorable terms. A finer lot of Mules is rarely offered to the public.

nov17—d:wtf   W. H. RIGHTER.

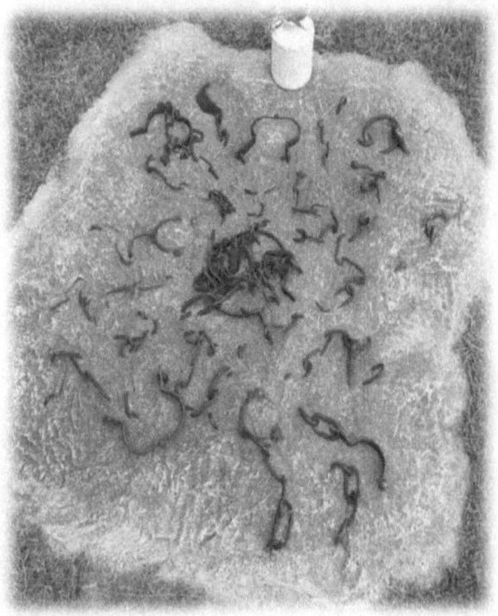

Natchez, Mississippi: Folks of the Road

Natchez, Mississippi: King's Tavern (1789) Mississippi Territory

Natchez, Mississippi: Longwood Plantation (1859), the largest
octagonal home in United States

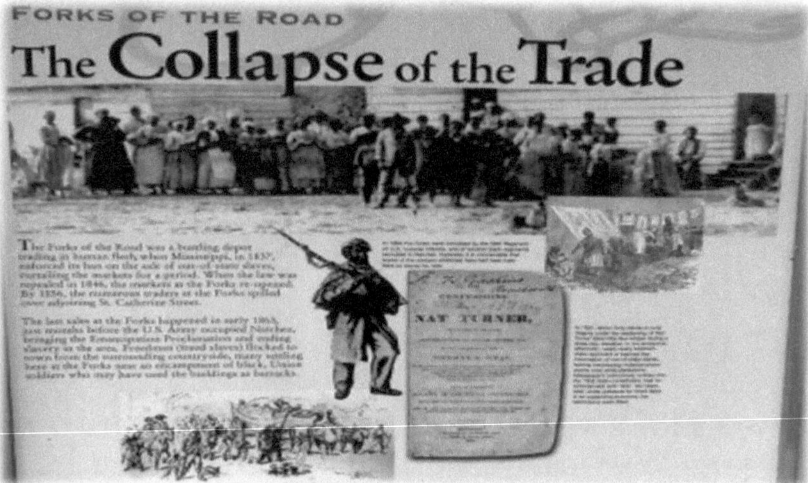

Natchez, Mississippi: Folks of the Road

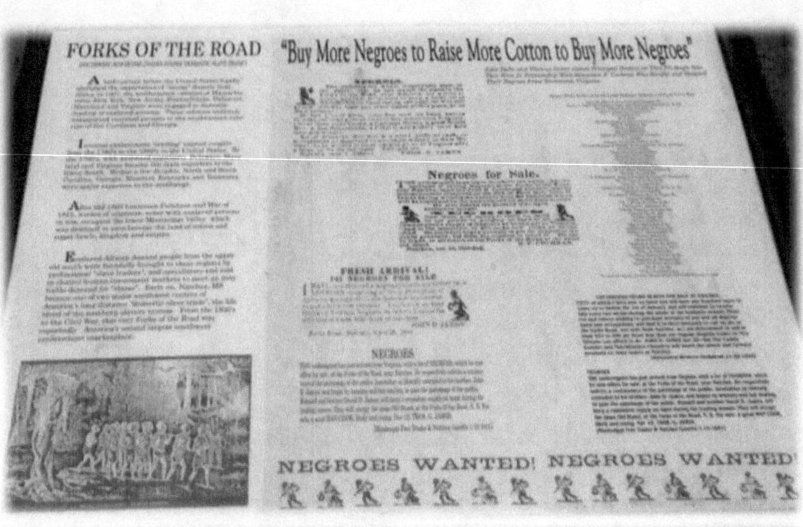

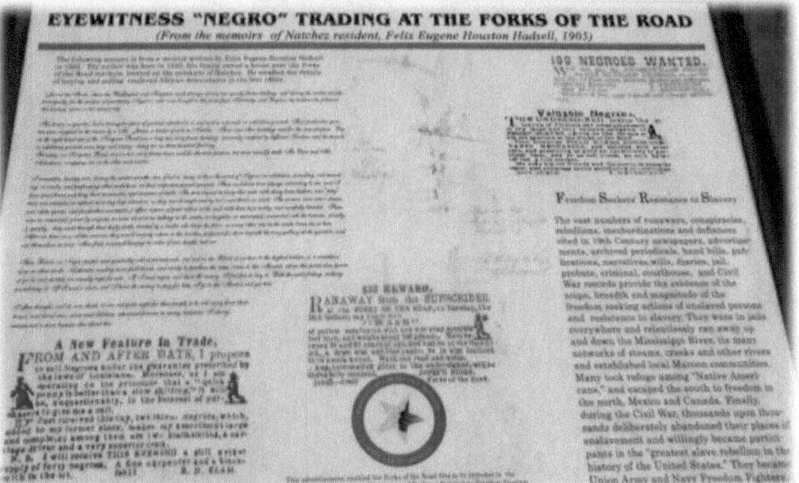

Natchez, Mississippi: Folks of the Road

Natchez, Mississippi: Folks of the Road

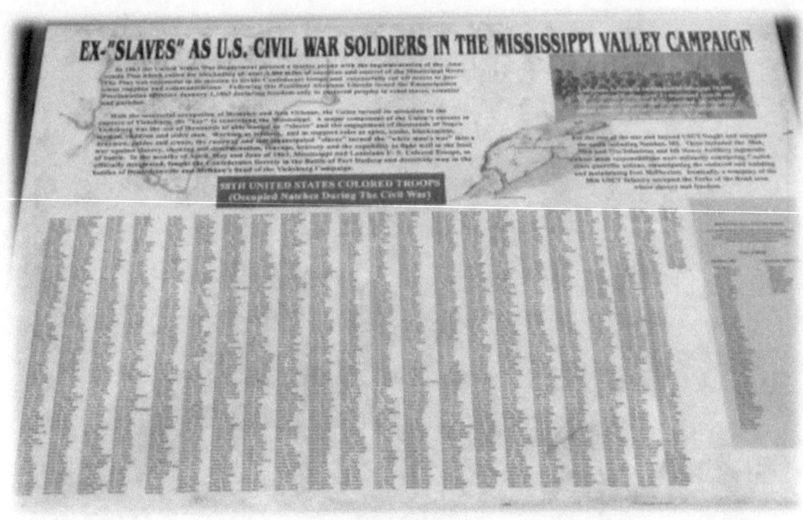

Natchez, Mississippi: Folks of the Road

Natchez, Mississippi: Natchez Village early 1800s in Mississippi

Mississippi: The process of picking cotton in Mississippi

Mississippi: Picking Cotton in Mississippi 1890

Jefferson Davis was a member of the United States House of
Representative and United States Senator for the state of
Mississippi. He became the president of the Confederate States of
America.

President of Confederate States of America from 1861 to 1865

Inauguration of Jefferson Davis as president of the Confederate
States of America in Montgomery, Alabama, in 1861.

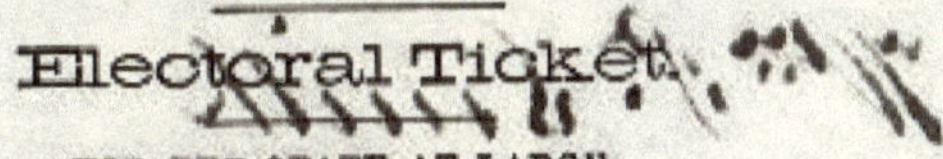

FOR PRESIDENT,
JEFFERSON DAVIS,
OF MISSISSIPPI.

FOR VICE-PRESIDENT,
ALEXANDER H. STEPHENS,
OF GEORGIA.

Electoral Ticket.

FOR THE STATE AT LARGE.
JOHN R. EDMUNDS, of Halifax.
ALLEN T. CAPERTON, of Monroe.

FOR THE DISTRICTS.

1st District—JOS. CHRISTIAN, of Middlesex.
2d District—CINCINNATUS W NEWTON, of Norfolk city
3d District—RALEIGH T. DANIEL, of Richmond city.
4th District—WM. F. THOMPSON, of Dinwiddie.
5th District—WOOD BOULDIN, of Charlotte.
6th District—WILLIAM L. GOGGIN, of Bedford.
7th District—BENJAMIN F. RANDOLPH, of Albemarle.
8th District—JAMES W. WALKER, of Madison.
9th District—ASA ROGERS, of Loudoun.
10th District—SAMUEL C. WILLIAMS, of Shenandoah.
11th District—SAMUEL McD. REID, of Rockbridge.
12th District—HENRY A. EDMUNDSON, of Roanoke.
13th District—JAMES W. SHEFFEY, of Smyth.
14th District—HENRY J. FISHER, of Mason.
15th District—JOS. JOHNSON, of Harrison.
16th District—E. H. FITZHUGH, of Ohio.

Bonnie Blue Mississippi Flag 1861. When Mississippi declared its secession from the Union on January 9, 1861, near the start of the American Civil War, spectators in the balcony handed a Bonnie Blue Flag down to the Secession Convention delegates on the floor,and one was raised over the capitol building in Jackson as a sign of independence.

 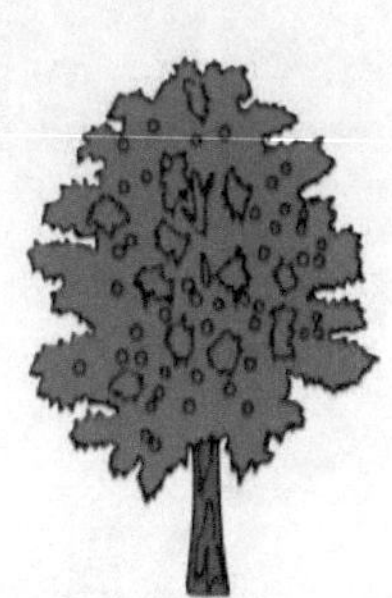 

The first official flag of Mississippi was known as the **Magnolia Flag**. It was the official flag of the state from 1861 until 1865. It remained in use as an unofficial flag until 1894, when the current state flag was first adopted.

The **flag of the state of Mississippi** was first adopted by the U.S. state of Mississippi in April 1894, replacing the unofficial flag that had been adopted in 1861 when Mississippi was a Confederate state. The flag was repealed in 1906 but remained in *de facto* use. When a referendum failed for a new design in April 2001, the state legislature voted to readopt the historic design that same month.

Mississippi the Magnolia State

Mississippi Coat of Arms

The Seal of Mississippi

Aberdeen, Mississippi: The Magnolias - 1850

Aberdeen, Mississippi: Adams - French Mansion - 1855

Aberdeen, Mississippi: The Old Homestead - 1852

The State of Mississippi

ABERDEEN

Formed 1834; chartered
1837; in 1849 it was made
county seat of Monroe, the
first county in the state
north of Vicksburg. Cotton
trade center and former
port for Mobile trade.

MAIN ST
ABERDEEN
MISS

River Plantation and Sharpley's Bottom

River Plantation and Sharpley's Bottom

Needham Whitfield, the first planter and slaveholder to own the River Plantation that would later be known as the Sharpley's Bottom, illustrates this early settlement development from the Slave Codes of Mississippi to the Black Codes of Mississippi. Whitfield from North Carolina moved to Aberdeen, Mississippi when the town was being chartered. Also from North Carolina, William B Sharpley is the second planter and slaveholder to own the property in which now is called Sharpley's Bottom.

Sharpley's Bottom is located in Monroe County, Mississippi, on the west bank of the Tombigbee River just south of the town of Aberdeen. It is the location of a large antebellum plantation which developed into a tenant farming community after the Civil War. The community at Sharpley's Bottom began and ended as a social unit organized with slave labor of the Africans (Negro) in which evolved into contract labor for the free slaves for the production of cotton. Agriculturally, it was tied to the rural dynamics of the Cotton South through the picking and exporting of the product worldwide for profit.

The Bottom is located in an isolated place. It is surrounded by water on three sides and is accessible by only one road leading going to Aberdeen. This isolation affected the lives of the people of Sharpley's Bottom, both as slaves and as tenant farmers. More than most, the people there did have a relatively isolated place in which to organize their own forms of social expression and to realize them in material culture forms. This isolation helped to build positive relationships with black community not having to dealt with a lot of outside white oppression behavior similar to the Lenoir Planation near Aberdeen in the prairie area. It was an isolation, however, which was sorely constrained by the economic condition of extreme poverty for the black.

Sharpley's Bottom, as a community, was spread out across the river bottomlands, to the hill on the west, along the road to Aberdeen and as far away as the James Creek Church. It included sites: houses, barns, a blacksmith shop, cotton gin, corn mill, sawmill, and churches, as well as features: roads, drainage ditches, artesian wells, a levee and a boat landing.

Historically

Chickasaw Indians *first* settled the land later known as Sharpley's Bottom in Monroe County, Mississippi. Although French and British traders had regular interaction with the Chickasaw Indians beginning in the late 17th century, sustained settlement by white Europeans in the upper Tombigbee Valley did not occur until the nineteenth century. European settlement increased following the conclusion of the 1816 land cession treaties with the Chickasaw and Choctaw Indians. As demand for Indian lands accelerated, and as territorial and federal authority exerted ever greater pressure on the Chickasaw, the Indians had little choice but to vacate their homeland. In the Treaty of Pontotoc, concluded between 1832 and 1834, they relinquished their homeland in exchange for land west of the Mississippi River.

The Europeans were concentrated in two principal areas in Mississippi – the Natchez District and the lower Tombigbee settlements above and west of Mobile. Approximately 4,500 people, including slaves, lived at Natchez, considerably more than the combined free and slave population of 1,250 that inhabited the Tombigbee settlements in 1800. Outside of these two areas, the territory was populated only by American Indians. The treaty launched a huge wave of new settlers to the area. Farmers with a dream of developing land in Mississippi came to this area of the South to covert the rich soils of the Tombigbee River bottoms and the fertile prairie lands west of the river. But people moved to the area paying for land for investing more quickly than the planters and held the choicest tracts even before public sales began in January 1836. Thereafter, land changed hands rapidly as newcomers found investing in land and selling it even more lucrative than cotton growing. A few settlers already lived in Mississippi when it was a Territory (Mississippi and Alabama).

River Plantation and Sharpley's Bottom

Needham Whitfield was born in North Carolina in 1791. He was a descendant from a rich and prominent family of farmers. After his father's death, he did not find a lot of ambitious opportunities in North Carolina. Whitfield's younger brother Gaius (already a thriving Alabama planter) urged him to move from North Carolina to the Alabama and Mississippi area. Gaius wrote that he was having good business in this area and he thought Needham would do well too.

By 1836, Needham Whitfield had taken his brother's advice and moved his family and most of his slaves to Monroe County, Mississippi. Once there, he purchased several thousand acres of farmland and numerous lots in the town of Aberdeen. Before 1840, he had acquired the Sharpley's Bottom tract from auctions and other purchases.

With Whitfield moving to Mississippi, it tied the cotton frontier with the seaboard plantation culture in North Carolina, and Needham Whitfield thus became the westernmost link in a chain of family that stretched from Mississippi to North Carolina for business. By 1840, one of Needham's brothers and two cousins moved their families to Monroe County. The western Whitfields in Mississippi acted as agents for their eastern family; in return, wealth and slaves went westward from North Carolina. These familial ties served Whitfield well between 1840 and 1860, while Monroe County developed from an outpost of white settlement into a prosperous plantation county with a sizable negro majority slave population.

Most settlers had moved with the plan of growing cotton, and they did so quickly. Cotton farming took varied forms according to the fertility of the land and the resources of the farmer. Small farmers worked plots with the labor of their own families and perhaps a few slaves. Large planters either used their slaves to clear and cultivate the land, or rented out all or part of their holdings to have them improved.

River Plantation and Sharpley's Bottom

Whitfield adopted the latter course in developing the Sharpley's Bottom tract, which he dubbed the "River Plantation" to distinguish it from his place on the prairie compared to many other plantation such as the "Lenoir Plantation". Cotton and slaves defined the plantation system that flourished on the bottomlands and fertile prairies of Monroe County.

The heavy labor necessities of cotton demanded increasing numbers of slaves. As a result, Monroe County's black population soared, growing three times as fast as the white population between 1830 and 1860 according to data from the 1872 United States Bureau of the Census. Slaves brought west with migrating masters or purchased from the seaboard slave states accounted for most of this rapid growth. Mississippi slaves, like their masters and the plantation system, had roots in the eastern seaboard states, a reality which any investigation of history, material culture, or conventional life must recognize.

The Slave Trail of Tears is the great missing migration in which a thousand-mile-long-river of people, all of them black, reaching from Maryland to Louisiana. During the 50 years before the Civil War, about a million enslaved people moved from the Upper South such as Virginia, Maryland, and Kentucky to the Deep South such as Alabama, Louisiana, and Mississippi. The slaves usually were moving with their slave masters; traveling for more opportunities with farming from the tobacco fields to the cotton fields of Mississippi.

The forced resettlement was 20 times larger than President Andrew Jackson's "Indian removal" campaigns of the 1830s, which gave rise to the original Trail of Tears as it drove tribes of Native Americans out of Georgia, Alabama, and Mississippi. It was bigger than the immigration of Jews into the United States during the 19th century when some 500,000 arrived from Russia and Eastern Europe. It was bigger than the migration to California. This movement lasted longer and grabbed up more people than any other migration in North

River Plantation and Sharpley's Bottom

America before 1900. The drama of a million negro slaves walking from their homes on the east seaboard plantation states changed the country. It gave the Deep South a character it retains today; and it changed the slaves themselves, traumatizing uncountable families within the dynamics of slavery. The "chain gang" has roots in the Slave Trail.

The experience of Needham Whitfield and his slaves indicates some of the ways in which the white slave master moved the Africa Negro slaves across the continent. Whitfield brought many of his family's slaves with him from North Carolina, but when he assumed operation of his own plantations in the early 1840s, he greatly enlarged his slave ownership. True to his speculative bent, he sold some slaves and bought many others. Although he purchased some of his new slaves from local slave traders according to the Monroe County Deed Book, most came into his possession through trade with family members.

River Plantation and Sharpley's Bottom

Through such dealings, Whitfield progressively increased the number of working-age slaves on his plantations. In 1840, he owned 47 slaves between the ages of 11 and 55. By the year 1860, Whitfield owned 65 slaves.

By about 1850, Whitfield's River Plantation had reached the physical shape that apparently changed little until after the Civil War. A road connecting Whitfield's town residence with a ferry across the Tombigbee ran through the northern end of the tract. The slave quarters were located between the road and the river. The plantation also contained cultivated fields, a cotton gin, corn mill, and other buildings. Also, the River Plantation was close to James Creek.

In 1856 the River Plantation had 300 of its approximately 1600 acres in cultivation for cotton mostly and corn with the slave doing the labor. The slaves lived on the plantation in the slave quarters. Whitfield's slaves almost certainly worked under the gang system, the typical plantation labor procedure in the cotton South. The presence of centralized slave quarters on the plantation and of two overseers residing with Whitfield's family in 1850s and 1860s, presumably one for each of his two plantations, lends credibility to this notion

The Civil War brought freedom to the slaves but left the slaves confused about their life, liberty, and independence from the practical sense of living life in America. The freed slaves were trying to maximize their independence from the white oppressive days of slavery. The **"Black Codes of Mississippi"** were formed by the state to lawfully re-impose the old dominion by the old white owners over the slaves. The battle was fought on many grounds, but the decisive struggle came over land and labor. As free labor replaced slavery as the organizing principle of plantation agriculture, both sides revealed much about their expectations of the

River Plantation and Sharpley's Bottom

new system in the negotiation of contracts. The struggle was hardly an equal one. The free slaves were subjected to laws that would send them to jail if they were not working under a contract by the first week of each month. The old slave masters held the balance of coercive power, but the freed slaves' ability to withhold their labor allowed them some leverage. Mostly all ex-slaves worked in one of three labor relationships: wage labor, sharecropping, or renting. Some ex-slaves obtained property but only a small number.

Wage labor was too similar to the antebellum gang system with an overseer; slaves did not prefer to work on old slave masters with labor relations. They objected to close white supervision and preferred to farm independently. The old white slave master resisted this but was willing to allow each black family to work its own tract of land with a house situated on it, in exchange for a large share of the crop. Sharecropping materialized as a compromise between old slaveholders for the plantation and freed slaves. While sharecropping offered advantages over wage labor, former slaves preferred rental tenure most of all: it posed greater risk than sharecropping however allowed -- tenants a larger control over crop mixture and cultivation methods, as well as greater chance of gaining in good years and enlarging their personal independence.

On Whitfield's River Plantation, standing rent, in which the tenant paid a specified amount of cotton rather than cash, became the main form of land contract labor relationship by 1868. In the spring of that year Whitfield made six contracts with ten tenants, all but one of them freedmen and women. The contracts assigned parcels of land ranging in size from 30 to 50 acres, for which Whitfield was to receive 32 and a half pounds of cotton per acre and 10 percent interest on all cash advanced to the tenants. A lien on the tenant's stock, personal property, and crop secured the agreement according to the Monroe County Deed Book. Whitfield and his tenants made and recorded such contracts - annually between 1868 and 1871.

River Plantation and Sharpley's Bottom

Over time, subtle alterations in the language of the contracts indicate profound changes in physical and social dealings that accompanied the post-emancipation transformation of River Plantation. For instance, the agreements reflected the tenants dissatisfaction with the physical entrapments of the old system of slavery. In 1868, the contracts described the rental tracts of land in relation to fields dating from the slavery era: the "potato patch," "Needham Field," "pea ridge." The freed slaves still lived in the central quarters, an indication of slavery. By 1870, however, the contracts made no mention of old fields or of the quarters; single household tenant cabins had replaced the slave quarters according to the Monroe County Deed Book.

Also, contracts revealed the composition of the tenant community and the renters' relations with Whitfield. In all likelihood, many of the black tenants (freed slaves) were descended from Whitfield's North Carolina slaves. Many of the ex-slaves took Whitfield's last name. Of the 14 tenants named Whitfield who made a contractual relationship with Needham Whitfield in one or more years between 1868 and 1872 and who also appeared in the 1870 census, all of them had been born in Mississippi or North Carolina, signifying that they had worked formerly among Whitfield's slaves and had perhaps labored on the River Plantation before emancipation according to the United States Census Manuscripts in Population for 1870.

Whitfield's former slaves composed the center of a black community which persisted despite the comings and goings of individual tenants. Familiar with the land and with the landlord (ex-Master), they possessed knowledge which sustained the community in the crucial years following emancipation. Such knowledge almost surely helped them win contract bargains from Whitfield, as in 1869, when the landlord lowered his tenants' rent and agreed not to raise it again if they repaired rundown fences and buildings according to the Monroe County Deed Book.

River Plantation and Sharpley's Bottom

The tenant community developed on Needham Whitfield's River Plantation in the early post slavery period changed considerably over the next 60 years. Behind a mask of outward stability, it moved to its own internal dynamic of life on the plantation, influenced by land tenure arrangements, the particulars of the landlord-tenant relationship, and the influence of community institutions such as families, schools, and churches.

Between 1868 and 1872, the tenant community entered a new stage when the aging **Whitfield** sold his **River Plantation** to **William B. Sharpley**, a North Carolinian who had moved to Monroe County around 1860 according to the Monroe County Deed Book. By that time he had learned the millwright's trade and purchased 15 slaves, one of whom, Si!vie. William had five mulatto daughters with Silvie. His bond with Silvie caused his wife of five years, Louisa Aberdeen Evans, to divorce him in 1865 according to the United States Census Manuscripts and Slave Population 1860.

One year after the divorce, Sharpley purchased a tract of land next to Whitfield's River Plantation. Shortly thereafter he began renting part of Whitfield's land and working it with black tenants, some of whom had previously been his slaves and others of whom had previously been slaves and tenants of Whitfield. In 1868, William purchased the piece of Whitfield's plantation he had been renting, and in 1872 acquired the rest of the property according to the Monroe County Deed. Between 1871 and 1875, William annually made tenant contracts similar to Whitfield's earlier agreements according to the Monroe County Deed Book and the Monroe County Deeds of Trust.

Comparably, the contracts of Whitfield and Sharpley constitute an unique source for the study of the ex-slaves staying at Sharley's Bottom. They demonstrate, first, that the ex-slaves there were a highly mobile group. A new

River Plantation and Sharpley's Bottom

landlord (or a falling-out with an old one), a better tenure arrangement elsewhere, the desire to unite with family or friends, and a host of other reasons could induce for ex-slaves moving to another plantation or just moving up North. The contracts also indicate that the majority of Sharpley's tenants remained renters with little or no property, victims of chronic debt, overworked soil, and periodic flooding of bottomlands. Although two of Sharpley's tenants managed by 1900 to climb the tenancy ladder to eventual land ownership, they were the exceptions according to the Depositions of Nat Whitfield and Jerry Harris from 1897-1901.

Unlike Whitfield before him, Sharpley lived on his plantation, and with home living on the property gave the community much of its distinctiveness in the Monroe County area of Mississippi for property owners of that generation. After Silvie's death in the early 1870s, Sharpley met Eva Tatum, a mulatto woman of mixed racial descent who had taught at the black school in the Bottom. They meet in Ohio when he sent his daughters to Oberlin College. They got married in Arkansas in 1879 at her father's place to avoid the racial scrutiny of Monroe County white people. She had three children with him before her death in 1886.

Sharpley was in constant violation of the long-established racial conventional lifestyle of the Southern white person not to build relationships with black more than less to have children and marry a Negro lady. He also had a positive relationship with his children. This placed Sharpley and his family in a world of their own living on his land. However, this set his family apart both from the Bottom's black tenants and from nearby whites. The physical shape of the Bottom embodied this social distance: Sharpley and his family resided on a hill west of the tenant fields in the sandy lowlands, away from the black tenants and isolated from whites by the natural cul-de-sac of the Bottom.

River Plantation and Sharpley's Bottom

Sharpley's death in 1888 wrought fundamental change in the tenant community. Two years earlier before his death, Sharpley had deeded a portion of his land to his three oldest daughters by Silvie and executed a will which retained the remainder in trust for his two surviving daughters by Eva Tatum according to the Monroe County Deed Book. The land willed to the oldest daughters continued to be farmed by rental tenants, similarly as it had been under the direction of Sharpley. The land held in trust was another story because in 1894 the land was dealings with legal issue. The land fell into the hands of John F. Plant, one of the wealthiest landlords in the county according to the Monroe County Deed Book. After a long-drawn-out lawsuit Sharpley's daughters recovered the land in 1902 (Sharpley, M., and L. Sharpley v. *J*. F. Plant 1897-1901), but Plant's tenure transformed both the physical landscape and the nature of the black community at the Bottoms.

Plant squeezed every conceivable profit from the Bottom; disregarding the future of the community and property. He hired a labor force to cut down the trees from the heavily forested riverbanks and cut down all the tall grass and canebrakes in the fields previously used to feed the tenants' livestock. He did not live on the property like Sharpley, Plant treated his tenants as cold-bloodedly and heartless. He visited the property once a week. Some tenants left when Plant began utilizing sharecroppers and seasonal wage laborers extensively. Plant had a difficulty getting tenant because of his tactics to the land and treatment of the ex-slaves tenants. In contrast, one of Sharpley's sons-in-law (Joe W. Tatum), who continued to offer rental tenures, reported no difficulty at all attracting tenants.

River Plantation and Sharpley's Bottom

The shifting away from using rental tenancy for the ex-slaves initiated by Plant was continued by H. S. Gilleylan who owned the large eastern section of the Bottom from 1904 until the early 1920s. Gilleylan wanted to maximize cotton production in the Bottom by requiring his tenants to plant more cotton and less food crops and by charging for use of garden plots and by the introduction of temporary day laborers. Commercial exploitation of timber resources was begun in the early 1900s, by Houston Gilleylan, who sold timber from the Bottom (Kern , 1982). In 1911, he sold the timber rights for the eastern portion of the Bottom to C. C. Day, who built and operated a saw-mill there. The saw-mill was no longer operating by 1923, when John Booth bought land in Sharpley's Bottom although the sawmill remains are visible today (Kern, 1982).

The controls which Gilleylan exacted were so harsh that by World War I none of his tenants in the Bottom had survived as renters (Kern, 1982). Thus during the first two decades of the twentieth century Gilleylan destroyed the social fabric of the Sharpley's Bottom rental tenant community which from Whitfield's time through Sharpley's had afforded blacks there a relative self-sufficiency and independence . After Gilleylan's tenure sharecroppers and day laborers worked the tract until disastrous flooding in 1927, the introduction of new sources of federal credit and farm modernization with using equipment in the 1930s, outmigration induced by wage labor opportunities during and after World War II, and the Cold War era transition to soybean farming as the new cash crop combined to spell the downfall of all forms of cotton tenancy in Sharpley's Bottom by the 1960s.

After Booth, Joe T. Morgan purchased the Bottoms. He was remembered as a popular man and politician. Again, the Bottoms had change a lot after Plant and Gilleylan. In time, the Bottoms would be called "Lovers Lane" because of the isolation by the Tombigbee River and James Creek. The Bottoms has a lot of history that helps us understand the Black Codes of Mississippi and the effects of the laws on the black communities (ex-slaves) in the United States of America.

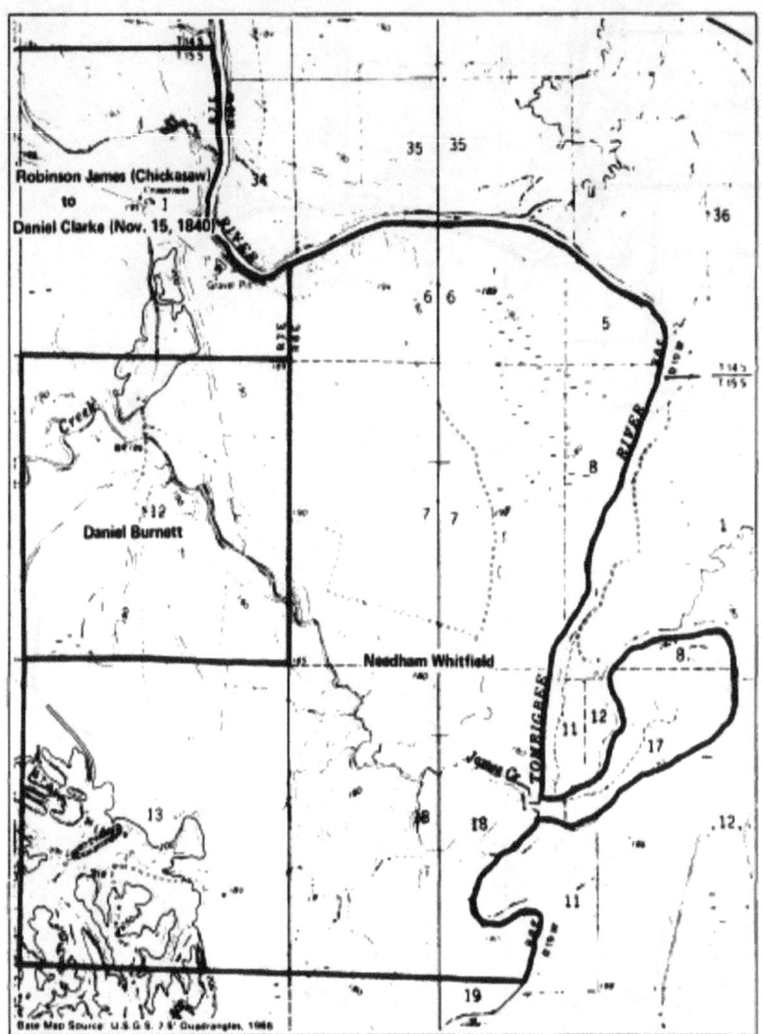

LAND OWNERSHIP 1840

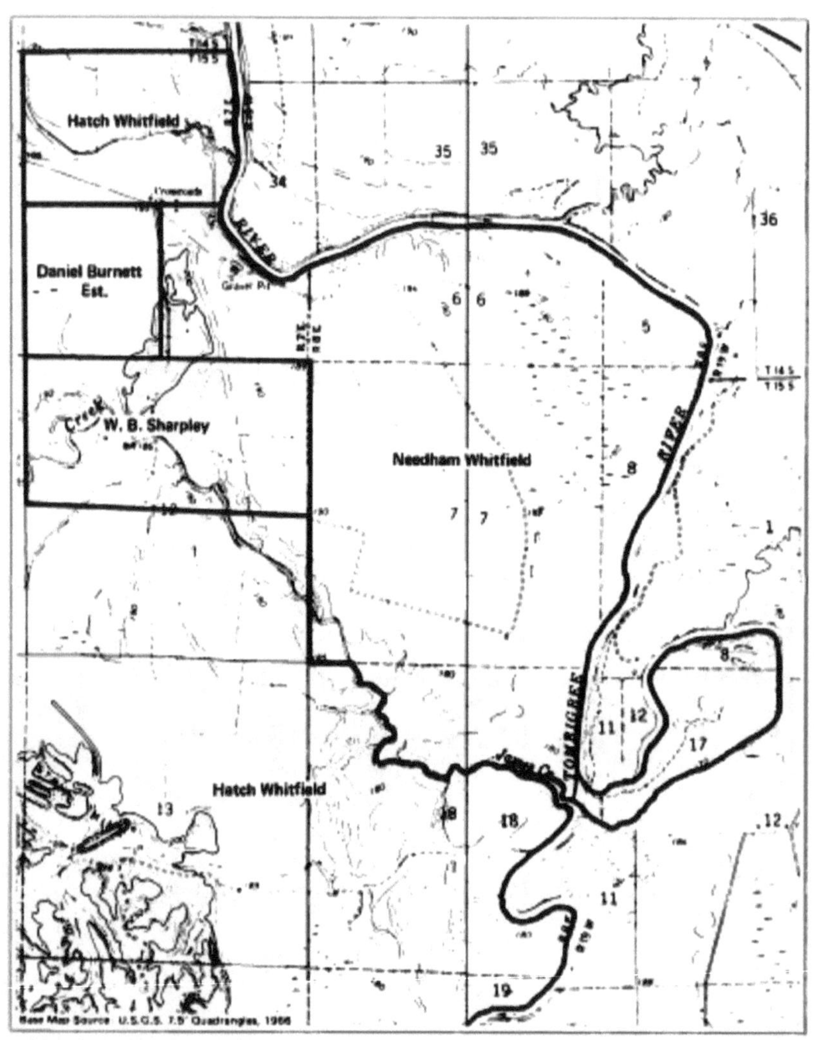

LAND OWNERSHIP – 1866

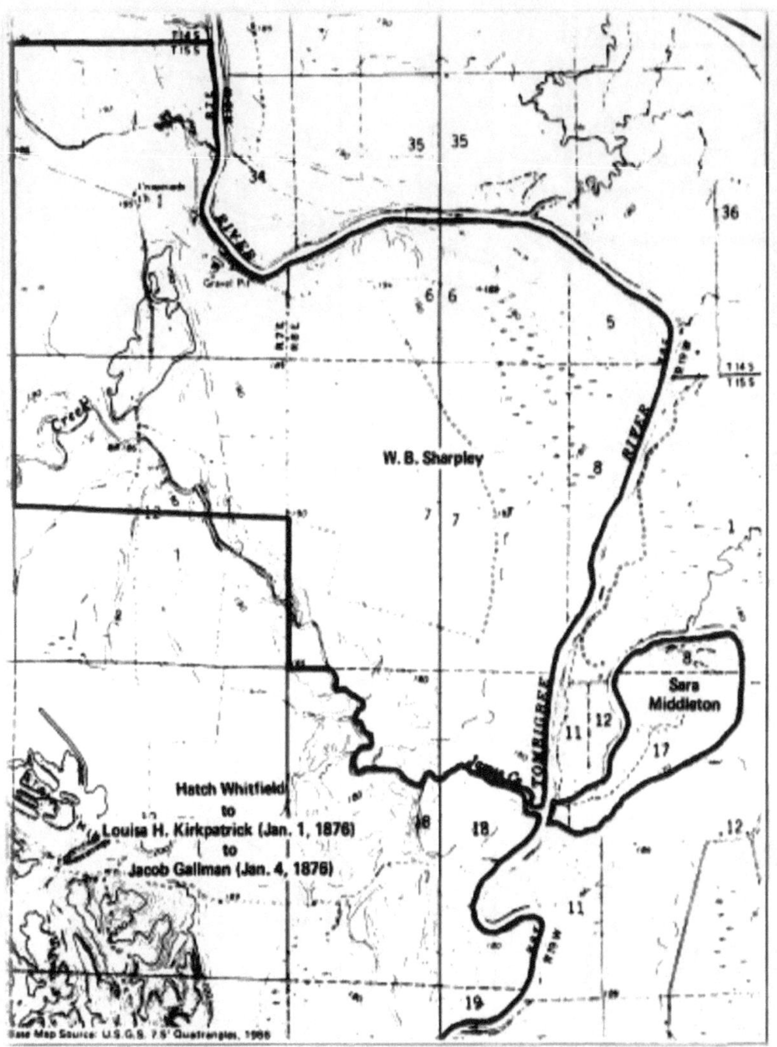

LAND OWNERSHIP - 1876

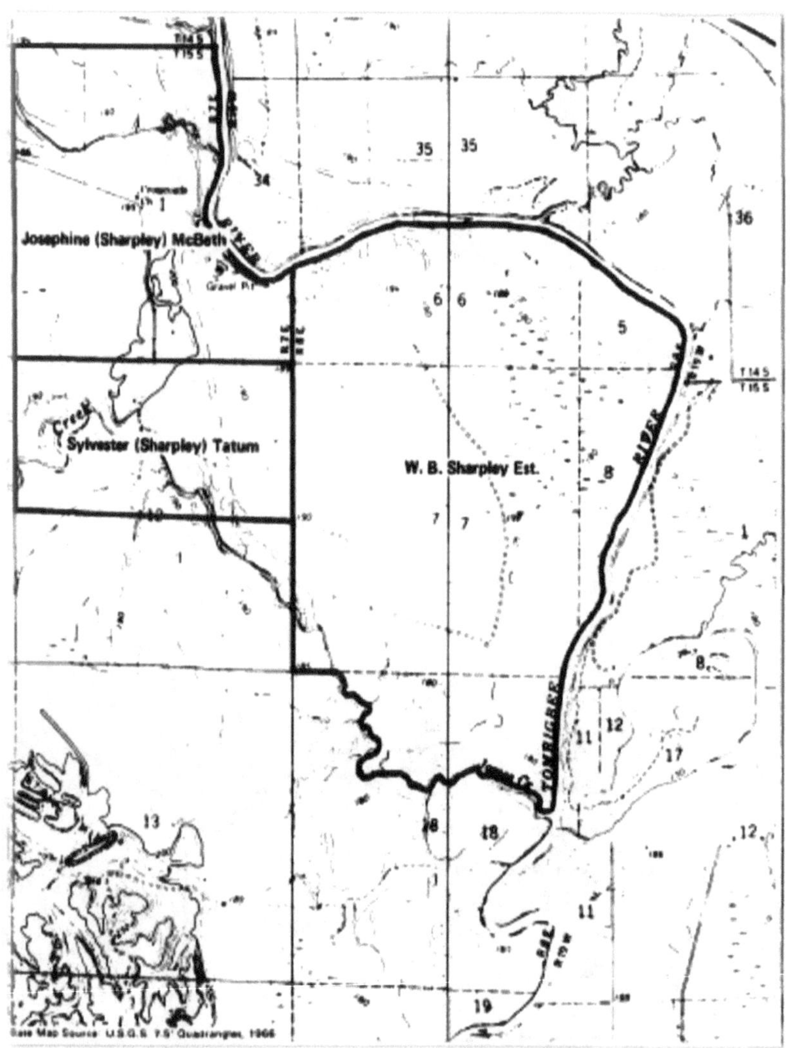

LAND OWNERSHIP - 1888

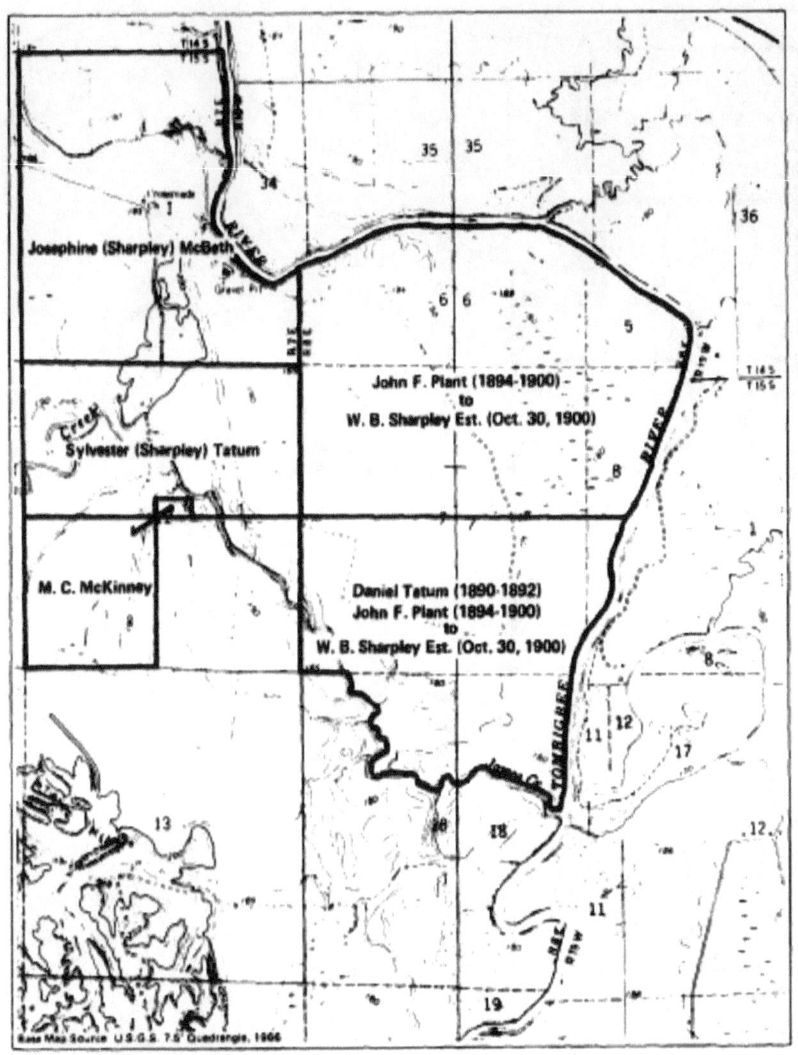

LAND OWNERSHIP – 1890 to 1900

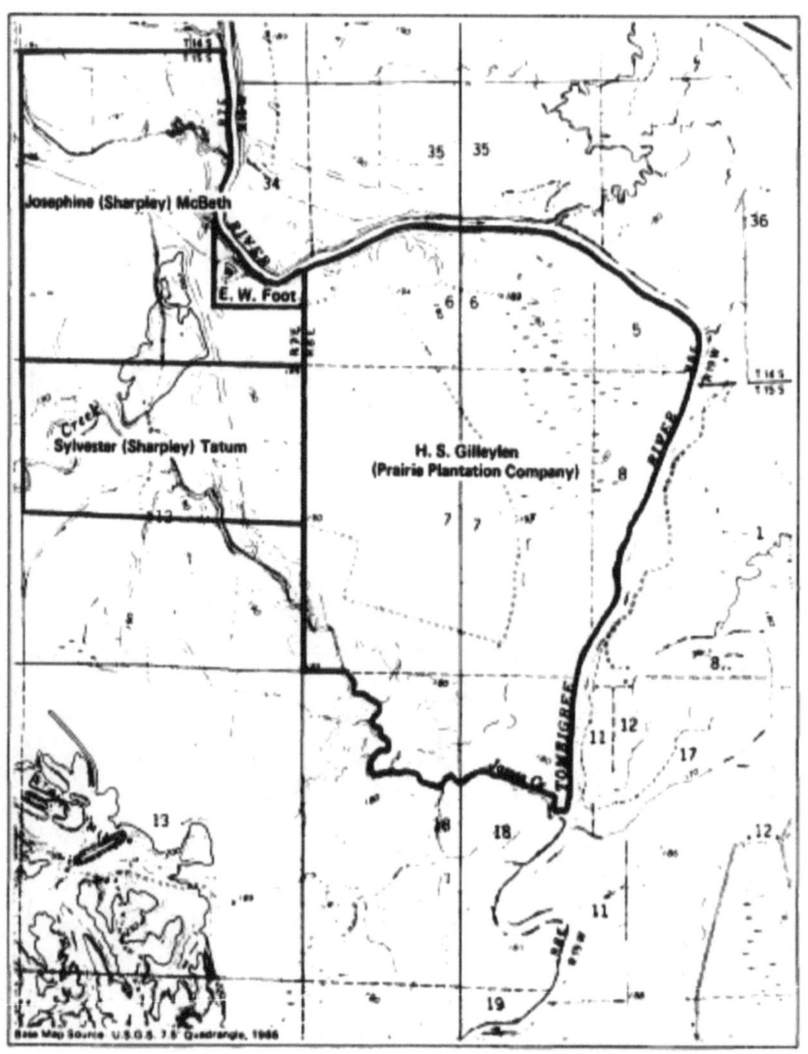

LAND OWNERSHIP – 1912

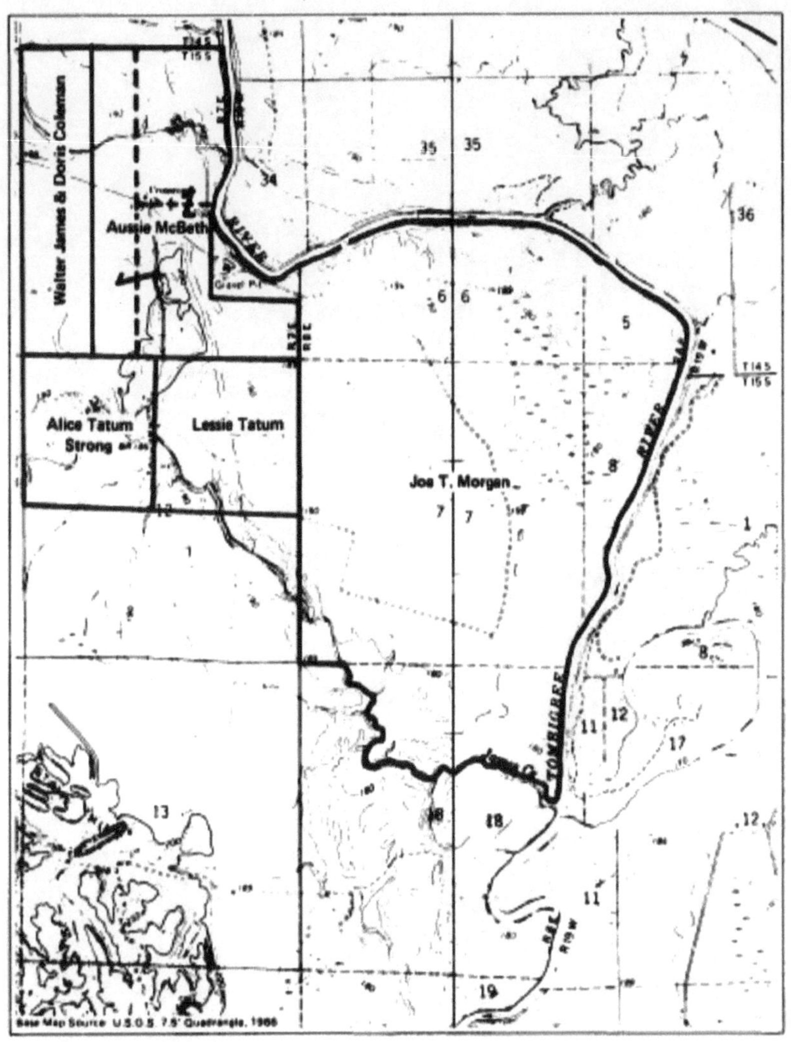

LAND OWNERSHIP – 1931

To The Public.

NEGROES BOUGHT AND SOLD.

Robert S. Adams & Moses J. Wicks have this day associated themselves under the name and style of Adams & Wicks, for the purpose of buying and selling Negroes, in the city of Aberdeen, 'and elsewhere. They have an Agent who has been purchasing Negroes for them in the Old States for the last two months. One of the firm, Robert S. Adams, leaves this day for North Carolina and Virginia, and will buy a large number of negroes for this market. They will keep at their depot in Aberdeen, during the coming fall and winter, a large lot of choice Negroes, which they will sell *low for cash*, or for bills on Mobile.

Robert S. Adams,
Moses J. Wicks.

Aberdeen, Miss., May 7th, 1852.

Ex-Slaves Narratives from Aberdeen, Mississippi

Louvenia Huff

"I was born third year after the surrender. There was thirteen children in my family when I was a child. We was different sizes and the grown children helped look after the little ones. My parents was field hands. My parents belong to Dr. Hatch. He lived in Aberdeen, Mississippi. We lived in the country on his place. He had five or six children. Ben and Needham come out to the farm. He was an old man and we stayed on the son's place — same place — till I come to Arkansas. We come in 1885. We heard it was a better country and open stock range. Dr. Hatch was very good to my folks.

"I don't think the Ku Klux bothered my folks but we was afraid of them.

"My father voted a Republican ticket. I never voted.

"My grandmother was real light skin. Mother was mixed with white. She told us she was sold away from her mother when she was a little bitter of a girl and never seen her no more till she was the mother of six children. They didn't know one another when they met. Her mother knowed who bought her and after freedom she kept asking about her and finally heard where she was and come to her. There was no selling place at Aberdeen so I don't know where she was bought. Dr. Hatch lived to be an old man. He owned a lot of slaves and lots of land.

Ex-Slaves Narratives from Aberdeen, Mississippi

"Father's old master was Whitfield. He sold him to Dr. Hatch when he was a young man. Father was a driver in the Civil War. He hauled soldiers and dumped them in the river. The Union soldiers wouldn't give them time to bury the other side. He took rations all but the times he hauled dead soldiers. He got shot in his arm above the wrist. He died before they give him a pension. He was a Union soldier. He talked a lot but that is all I can tell straight. I don't know if he mustered out or not.

"I worked in the field, wash, iron, and cooked. We get $12 from the Welfare. My husband had two strokes. He has been sick three years.

"My parents' name Simpson Hatch and Jacob Hatch. They had thirteen children."

<u>Richard Crump, Jr.</u>

"I was born right here in Aberdeen, Mississippi about five miles from the town on the east side of the Tom Bigbee River in Monroe County, Mississippi.

"My father's name was Richard Crump. My mother was named Emily Crump. My grandmother on my father's side was named Susan Crump. My mother came from Middleton, Tennessee. But I don't know nothing about any of her people. My father said he come from South Carolina when he was a boy eight or ten years old. That was way before I was born. They brought him to Mississippi from South Carolina.

"My father's master was old man Johnnie Crump. My mistress was named Nina Crump. That was Johnnie Crump's wife. My mars had four boys to my remembrance. One was named Wess, one was named Rufe, one was named Joe, and one was named Johnnie. He had a girl named Annie and one named Lulu.

"My mother was the mother of thirteen children. I am the onliest one living, that I know of. The way they gwine with us now, I ain't goin' a be here long. Just got four dollars to pay rent and bills and git somethin' to eat for a month. You don't git nothin' much when you git the commodities—no grease to cook with.

"We never had no trouble much when I was coming along. My mars was a pretty good old man. He didn't allow no overseer to whip his slaves.

Ex-Slaves Narratives from Aberdeen, Mississippi

The overseer couldn't whip my old mother anyhow because she was a kind of
bully and she would git back in a corner with a hoe and dare him in. And he
wouldn't go in neither.

"My grandmother had three or four sons. One was name Mele Crump,
another was named Miles and another was named Henry and another Jim. She had
two or three more but I can't think of them. They died before I was old
enough to know anything. Then she had two or three daughters. One was named
Lottie. She had another one but I can't think of her name. I was so little.
All of them are dead now. All of my people are dead but me. They are trying
to find a sister of mine, but I ain't found her yet. She oughter be down here
by Forrest City somewheres. But there ain't nobody here that I know about but
me. And the way they're carryin' them now I ain't goin' to be here long. All
of them people you hear me talk about, they're supposed to be dead.

"I was born in 1858. At least the old man told me that. I mean my
father of course. The first thing I knowed anything about was picking cotton.
I was a little bitty old fellow with a little sack hangin' at my side. I was
pickin' beside my mother. They would grab us sometimes when we didn't pick
right. Shake us and pull our ears.

"I didn't know anything about sellin' and buying. I never was sold.

"The next thing I remember was being told I was free. My daddy said old
mars told them they were free. I didn't hear him tell it myself. They come
'round on a Monday morning and told papa and the rest that they were free as
he was and that they could go if they wanted to or they could stay, 'cause
they were free as he was and didn't have no master no more, didn't have no
one to domineer over them no more.

"Right after freedom, my folks worked on old man Jim Burdyne's farm. That
is the first place I remember after freedom. Father taken a little deadening.

You don't know what a deadening is? That's a lease. He cleaned up some land. We boys were just gettin' so we could pick up brush and tops of trees—and burn it, and one thing and another. Two years after the War was over, I got big enough to plow. I was plowing when I was nine years old. We had three boys and four girls older than me. The balance of them was born after freedom. We made crops on shares for three years after freedom, and then we commenced to rent. Shares were one-third of the cotton and one-fourth of the corn. They didn't pay everything they promised. They taken a lot of it away from us. They said figures didn't lie. You know how that was. You dassent dispute a man's word then. Sometimes a man would get mad and beat up his overseer and run him away. But my daddy wouldn't do it. He said, 'Well, if I owe anything I'll pay it. I got a large family to take care of.'

"I never got a chance to go to school any. There was too much work to do. I married when I was twenty-one. I would go off and stay a month or two and come back. Never left home permanent for a long while. Stayed 'round home till I was forty years old. I come to Arkansas in 1896. I made a living by farming at first.

"I didn't shoot no craps. I belong to the church. I have belonged to the church about forty years or more. I did play cards and shoot craps and things like that for years before I got religion.

"I come to Little Rock in 1918 and been here ever since. I worked 'round here in town first one thing and then another. Worked at the railroad and on like that.

"We used to vote right smart in Mississippi. Had a little trouble sometimes but it would soon die down. I haven't voted since I been here. Do no good nohow. Can't vote in none of these primary elections.

Ex-Slaves Narratives from Aberdeen, Mississippi

Vote for the President. And that won't do no good. They can throw your
ballot out if they want to.

"I believe in the right thing. I wouldn't believe in anything else. I
try to be loyal to the state and the city. But colored folks don't have
much show. Work for a man four or five years and go back to him and he
don't know nothin' about you. They soon forget you and a white man's word
goes far.

"I was able to work as late as 1930, but I ain't been no 'count since
to do much work. I got a pension for old age from the Welfare and commodities and I depend on that for a living. Whatever they want to give me,
I'll take it and make out with it. If there's any chance for me to git a
slave's pension, I wish they would send it to me. For I need it awful bad.
They done cut me way down now. I got heart trouble and high blood pressure
but I don't give up.

"My mother sure used to make good ash cake. When she made it for my
daddy, she would put a piece of paper on it on top and another on the bottom.
That would keep it clean. She made it extra good. When he would git through,
she would give us the rest. Sometimes, she wouldn't put the paper on it
because she would be mad. He would ask, 'No paper today?' She would say,
'No.' And he wouldn't say nothin' more.

"There is some of the meanest white people in the United States in
Mississippi up there on the Yellow Dog River. That's where the Devil makes
meanness.

"There's some pretty mean colored folks too. There is some of them
right here in Little Rock. Them boys from Dunbar give me a lot of trouble.
They ride by on their bicycles and holler at us. If we say anything
to them, they say, 'Shut up, old gray head.' Sometimes they say worse.

Ex-Slaves Narratives from Aberdeen, Mississippi

I used to live by Brother Love. Christmas the boys threw at the house and gave me sass when I spoke to them. So I got out of that settlement. Here it is quiet because it is among the white folks."

Dora Franks

Dora Franks, ex-slave, lives at Aberdeen, Monroe County.
She is about five feet tall and weighs 100 pounds. Her hair is in-
clined to be curly rather than kinky. She is very active and does
most of her own work.

"I was born in Choctaw County, but I never knowed zackly
how old I was, 'cause none o' my folks could read an' write. I
reckon I be's 'bout a hund'ed, 'cause I was a big girl long time
fo' Surrender. I was old 'nough to marry two years after dat.

"My mammy come from Virginny. Her name was Harriet Brewer.
My daddy was my young Marster. His name was Marster George Brewer
an' my mammy always tol' me dat I was his'n. I knew dat dere was
some dif'ence 'tween me an' de res' o' her chillun, 'cause dey was
all coal black, an' I was even lighter dan I is now. Lawd, it's
been to my sorrow many a time, 'cause de chillun used to chase me
'round an' holler at me, 'Old yellow Nigger.' Dey didn' treat me
good, neither.

"I stayed in de house mos' o' de time wid Miss Emmaline.

Miss Emmaline's hair was _dat_ white, den I loved her 'cause she was so good to me. She taught me how to weave an' spin. 'Fore I was bigger'n a minute I could do things dat lots o' de old han's couldn' come nigh doin'. She an' Marse Bill had 'bout eight chillun, but mos' of 'em was grown when I come 'long. Dey was all mighty good to me an' wouldn' 'low nobody to hurt me.

"I 'members one time when dey all went off an' lef' me wid a old black woman call Aunt Ca'line what done de cookin' 'round de place some o' de time. When dey lef' de house I went in de kitchen an' asked her for a piece o' white bread lak de white folks eat. She haul off an' slap me down an' call me all kin' o' names dat I didn' know what dey meant. My nose bled an' ruint de nice clean dress I had on. When de Mistis come back Marse George was wid 'er. She asked me what on earth happen to me an' I tol' 'er. Dey call Ca'line in de room an' asked her if what I say was de truf. She tell 'em it was, an' dey sent 'er away. I hear tell dat dey whup her so hard dat she couldn' walk no mo'.

"Us never had no big fun'als or weddin's on de place. Didn' have no marryin' o' any kin'. Folks in dem days jus' sorter hitched up together an' call deyse'ves man an' wife. All de cullud folks was buried on what dey called Platnum Hill. Dey didn' have no markers nor nothin' at de graves. Dey was jus' sunk in places. My brother Frank showed me once where my mammy was buried. Us didn' have no preachin', or singin', or nothin', neither. Us didn' even git to have meetin's on Sund'y less us slip off an' go to some other plantation. Course, I got to go wid de white folks sometime an' set in de back, or on de steps. Dat was when I was little.

"Lots o' Niggers would slip off from one plantation to de other to see some other Niggers. Dey would always manage to git back 'fore daybreak. De wors' thing I ever heard 'bout dat was once when my Uncle Alf run off to 'jump de broom.' Dat was what dey called goin' to see a woman. He didn' come back by daylight, so dey put de Nigger hounds after 'im. Dey smelled his trail down in de swamp an' foun' where he was hidin'.

"Now, he was one o' de biggest Niggers on de place an' a powerful fas' worker. But dey took an' give him 100 lashes wid de cat o' ninety-nine tails. His back was somethin' awful, but dey put him in de fiel' to work while de blood was still a-runnin'. He work right hard 'til dey lef'. Den, when he got up to de end o' de row nex' to de swamp, he lit out ag'in.

"Dey never foun' 'im dat time. Dey say he foun' a cave an' fix him up a room whar he could live. At nights he would come out on de place an' steal enough t'eat an' cook it in his little dugout. When de war was over an' de slaves was freed, he come out. When I saw him, he look lak a hairy ape, 'thout no clothes on an' hair growin' all over his body.

Dem was pretty good days back in slav'ry times. My Marster had a whole passel o' Niggers on his place. When any of 'em would git sick dey would go to de woods an' git herbs an roots an' make tea for 'em to drink. Hogweed an' May apples was de bes' things I knowed of. Sometimes old Mistis doctored 'em herse'f. One time a bunch o' us chillun was playin' in de woods an foun' some o' dem May apples. Us et a lot of 'em an' got awful sick. Dey dosed us up on grease an' Samson snake root to clean us out. An' it sho' done a good job. I'se been a-usin' dat snake root ever since.

"De firs' thing dat I 'member hearin' 'bout de war was one day when Marse George come in de house an' tell Miss Emmaline dat dey's gwine have a bloody war. He say he feared all de slaves 'ud be took away. She say if dat was true she feel lak jumpin' in de well. I hate to hear her say dat, but from dat minute I started prayin' for freedom. All de res' o' de women done de same.

"De war started pretty soon after dat an' all de men folks went off an' lef' de plantation for de women an' de Niggers to run. Us seen de sojers pass by mos' ever'day. Once de Yankees come an' stole a lot o' de horses an' somp'in' t'eat. Dey even took de trunk full o' 'Federate money dat was hid in de swamp. How dey foun' dat us never knowed.

"Marse George come home 'bout two years after de war started an' married Miss Martha Ann. Dey had always been sweethearts. Dey was promised 'fore he lef'.

"Marse Lincoln an' Marse Jeff Davis is two I 'members 'bout. But, Lawzee! Dat was a long time back. Us liked Marse Jeff Davis de bes' on de place. Us even made up a song 'bout him, but, I 'clare 'fore goodness, I can't even 'member de firs' line o' dat song. You see, when I got 'ligion, I asked de Lawd to take all de other songs out o' my head an' make room for his word.

"Since den it's de hardes' thing in de worl' for me to 'member de songs us used to dance by. I do 'member a few lak 'Shoo, Fly', 'Old Dan Tucker', an' 'Run, Nigger, Run, de Pateroller Catch You.' I don' 'member much o' de words. I does 'member a little o' 'Old Dan Tucker.' It went dis way:

> 'Old Dan Tucker was a mighty mean man,
> He beat his wife wid a fryin' pan.
> She hollered an' she cried, "I's gwineter go,
> Dey's plenty o' men, won't beat me so."
>
> 'Git out o' de way, Old Dan Tucker,
> You come too late to git yo' supper.
>
> 'Old Dan Tucker, he got drunk,
> Fell in de fire, kicked up a chunk,
> Red hot coal got down his shoe
> Oh, Great Lawd, how de ashes flew.
>
> 'Git out o' de way, Old Dan Tucker,
> You come too late to git yo' supper.'

"When de war was over, my brother Frank slipped in de house where I was still a-stayin'. He tol' me us was free an' for me to come out wid de res'. 'Fore sundown dere warnt one Nigger lef' on de place. I hear tell later dat de Mistis an' de gals had to git out an' work in de fiel's to he'p gather in de crop.

"Frank foun' us a place to work an' put us all in de fiel'. I never had worked in de fiel' before. I'd faint away mos' ever'day 'bout eleven o'clock. It was de heat. Some of 'em would have to tote me to de house. I'd soon come to. Den I had to go back to de fiel'. Us was on Marse Davis Cox's place den.

"Two years later I met Pet Franks an' us married. De Cox's was good folks an' give us a big weddin'. All de white folks an' de Niggers for miles a-round come to see us git married. De Niggers had a big supper an' had a peck t'eat. Us had eight chillun, but aint but three of 'em livin'. Me an' Pet aint been a-livin' together for de las' twenty-three years. Us jus' couldn' git 'long together, so us quit. He lives out at Acker's Fishing Lodge now an' does de cookin' for 'em.

"I never will forgit de Klu Klux Klan. Never will I forgit de way dat horn soun' at night when dey was a-goin' after some mean Nigger. Us'd all run an' hide. Us was livin' on de Troup place den, near old Hamilton, in one o' de brick houses back o' de house whar dey used to keep de slaves. Marse Alec Troup was one o' de Klu Klux's an' so was Marse Thad Willie dat lived close by. Dey'd make plans together sometime an' I'd hear 'em. One time dey caught me lis'nin', but dey didn' do nothin' to me, 'cause dey knowed I warnt gwine tell. Us was all good Niggers on his place.

"Lawd, Miss, dese here young folks today is gwine straight to de Devil. All dey do all day an' all night is run 'round an'

drink corn likker an' ride in automobiles. I'se got a grand-daughter
here, an' she's dat wil'. I worries a right smart 'bout her, but
it dont do no good, 'cause her mammy let her do jus' lak she please
anyhow.

"Den I tells you de one thing I worries 'bout mos': Dat
is de white folks what lives here 'mongst de Niggers. You know what
kinda folks dey is, an' it sho' is bad influence on 'em. You knows
Niggers aint s'posed to always know de right from de wrong. Dey
aint got Marsters to teach 'em now. For de white folks to come down
here an' do lak dey do, I tells you, it aint right. De quality white
folks ought-a do somethin' 'bout it.

"I's had a right hard life, but I puts my faith in de Lawd
an' I know ever'thing gwine come out all right. I's lived a long
life an' will soon be a hund'ed, I guess. I's glad dat slav'ry is
over, 'cause de Bible don't say nothin' 'bout it bein right. I's a
good Christian. I gits sort-a res'less mos' o' de time an' has to
keep busy to keep from thinkin' too much."

<u>Wayne Holliday</u>

"I was born an' raised in Aberdeen an' I'se been a railroed nigger fo' mos' of my days. I'se retired now 'cause dey say I too old to work any longer, but shucks, I ain't half dead yet. I was born in 1853 right here close to whar I live now. My folks b'longed to de Hollidays -- you know de grand folks of Miss Maria Evans? An' we stayed right dere in de lot whar de white folks lived.

"My pa an' my ma was named Frank an' Sarah Holliday an' de Cunel brung dem wid him frum North Car'lina. Dey was lot niggers an' never worked in de fiel' or lived in de Quarters. My pa was one of de best carpenters in de country. I was too young to work much but sometime I he'ped him 'roun' de house but mos' of de time, I jes played wid my brudders an' sisters an' de white chullun what lived aroun'. We played marbles, ridin' de stick hoss, an' play house jes lak de chullun do now days, but I think we had mo' fun. Dey was fo'teen of us in our family an' we allus had somebody to play wid. An' den li'l Marse Ben, he wa'nt much older dan us.

"Our marster's name was Cunel John Holiday. He got dat title in a war before de slav'ry war. He was too old to fight in dat one, or I spect he'd got another title, lak Gen'ral or somethin'. He an' Miss Julia - dat was his wife - was mighty good to us an' so was Marse Tom and Marse Ben, an' Miss Maria an' all. When de Cunel fust come to Mississippi he bought a plantation in de prairies an' lived dere for a while. But later he 'cided to build him a house in town so he got my pa to he'p him build it an' it was one of de purtiest houses in Aberdeen. It look jes lak it allus did to me now. Co'se dey is worked on it several times since den, but dey ain't changed it at all.

"My mammy did de cookin' for de white folks dere. Dey all thought a lot of her. I never knowed much wh t slav'ry was 'bout, to tell de truf. De folks never treated us wrong an' chullun in dem days didn' get to run aroun' lak dey do today an' we didn' get to hear no gossip 'bout de other niggers. Since we didn' live in no quarters we didn' hear nothin. Our folks never said nothin' 'cause day was very well satisfied lak dey was. We never hear of no whuppin's, or runaways either, 'til afte' de War an' when we got older.

"I 'member de War tho'. Marse Tom, he went fust, wid de Van Dorns. He was made a capt'in or somethin' 'cause he was so brave. He fought long wid de fust an' was one of de fust to get hit. Dey brung his body all de way from Richmond, or Virginny, I fergit which, and lawzy, if de Cunel an' de Miss didn' take on somethin' awful. Dey sho' loved dat boy an' so did all of de niggers. Afte' dey buried him dey took his sword an' hung it on de wall of de parlor. I reckin it still dar.

"Marse Ben went afte' dat. He was jes old 'nough to go but he went an' fought jes de same. He come back when de war was over an' dey was sho' some rejoicin'. ¬

"Time wa'nt much diffrunt den dan it was 'fo de War. We stayed on wid our folks for a long time. Den my pa started gettin' a li'l work here an' dar an' purty soon he got all his chullun started out purty well. We all went to de colored school what dey had down whar de railroad crossin' is now, an' dat was whar I l'arned to read an' write. I didn' marry for a good while an' den I went to work on de I.C. Railroad. I was fust a coal heaver an' den a coach porter. I was faithful to my job an' made good money an' soon built me a house of my own whar I raised my family. I sent all my chullun to school an' dey is doin' well. My wife worked right 'long wid me. She died 'bout two years ago.

"I'se thankful I ain't got no sad mem'ries 'bout slav'ry times an' dat I an' my folks is done as well as dey have. T'is de work of de Lawd."

Wayne Holliday, who lived in slavery times, and whose father was a slave, is 84 years old, a dried-up looking Negro of

light tan color. Approximately 5 feet three inches high and weigh-
ing about 130 pounds, he is most active and appears much younger
than he really is. He is slightly bent; his kinky hair is inter-
mingled white and gray; and his broad mouth boasts only one
visible tooth, a particularly large one in the extreme center of
his lower gum.

Wayne has the manner of a Negro of the old South and
depicts, in his small way, the gallantry of an age gone by.

Cecil Copeland

"I wuz born March 15, 1843, in Monroe County, Mississippi, near Aberdeen, Mah Mahster wuz Colonel Ogburn, one ob de bigges' planters in de state of Miss- issippi. Manys de time he raised so much cotton dat dem big steamers just could- nt carry it all down to N'Awlins in one year. But den along came de Civil War an' we didn't raise nothin' fo' several years. Why? Becase most uf us jined th Confederate Army in Colonel Ogburn's regiment as servants and bodyguards. An' let me tell yo' somethin', whitefolks. Dere never wuz a war like dis war. Why I 'member dat after de battle of Corinth, Miss., a five acre field was so thickly covered wid de dead and wounded dat yo' couldn't touch de ground in walkin' across it. And de onliest way to bury dem wuz to cut a deep furrow wid a plow, lay de soldiers head to head, an' plow de dirt back on dem."

Charles Grandy

Charles Grandy was born February 19, 1842, in Mississippi. While still an infant, he was brought to Norfolk. When the family arrived in Norfolk his father was arrested on some pretentious charge, and the whole family was placed in prison. After their release , they were taken to a plantation near Hickory Ground, Virginia, and sold. Slaves, at this time, were often taken to rural districts in carts, and sold to owners of plantations, as they were needed. Family life, friendships, and love affairs were often broken up; many times never to be united.

Following the general routine of slaves, the Grandy family was given a shanty; food and clothing was also issued to them, and had to last until the master decided to give out another supply. Usually, he issued them their allowance of food weekly. Often the supply was insufficient for their needs.

Charles played around the plantation "big house", doing small errands until he reached the age of five, then his play days ended. While playing on the wood pile one morning, his master called him, "boy do you see this grass growing along the side of the fence? Well pull it al up." When his first task was finished, he was carried to the field to pull the grass from the young cotton and other growing crops. This work was done by hand because he was still too young to use the farm implements. Now he want to his task daily; from early in the morning until late in the evening. The long toilsome days completely exhausted the youngster. Often he would fall asleep before reaching home, and spend a good portion of the night on the bare ground. Awakening, he would find it quite a problem to locate his home in the darkness of night.

From the stage of grass pulling by hand, he grew strong enough, in a few years, to use the hoe rake and sickle. While attempting to carry out his masters orders to cut corn tassels with a large sharp knife, his elbow was seriously cut. He was taken to the house and treated, the application being chimmey soot, to stop the bleeding. After this treatment the arm was placed in a sling, and eventually became deformed from insufficient care. He was sent back to the fields to pick cotton, with one free hand and his teeth, while painfully carrying the other hand in the sling. Failing to obey this command, he would have been given a whipping, or sent to the southlands. Sending slaves to the plantations of Mississippi and other southern states was a type of punishment all slaves feared.

Slaves were not allowed much freedom of worship. The Yankee soldiers and officers played a great part in the slave's moral training, and religious worship. They secretly instructed small gatherings of slaves, at night. The points stressed most were, obedience and the evils of stealing. There were some sections where masters were liberal in their views toward their slaves, and permitted them to worship openly.

Slaves were allowed to have small quantities of whiskey, even during the days of their worship, to use for medicinal purposes. It was a common occurrence to see whiskey being sold at the foot of the hill near the churchyard.

The news of war, and the possibility of Negroes enlisting as soldiers was truly a step closer to the answering of their prayers for freedom. Upon hearing of this good news Grandy joined a few of the others in this break for freedom. One night, he and a close friend packed a small quantity of food in a cloth and set out about midnight to join the northern army. Traveling at night most of the time, they were constantly confronted with the danger of being recaptured. Successfully eluding their followers, they reached Portsmouth after many narrow escapes. From Portsmouth they moved to Norfolk.

Arriving in Norfolk, Grandy and his friend decided to take different roads of travel. Several days and nights found him wandering about the outskirts of Norfolk, feeding on wild berries, etc. While picking berries along a ditch bank, he was hailed by a Yankee soldier, who having come in contact with run away slaves before, greeted him friendly, and questioned him of his home and of his knowledge of work. He was taken to camp and assigned as cook. At first, he was not very successful in his job, but gradually improvement was shown. He was asked what wages he would accept. It was such a pleasure to know that he had escaped the clutches of slavery, he did not ask for wages; but instead, he was willing to work for anything they would give him, no matter how small, as long as he didn't have to return to slavery.

Within a short period he was given a uniform and gun; was fully enlisted as a soldier, in the 19th regiment of Wisconsin, Company E. Here he remained in service until November, 1862, after which time he returned to Norfolk to spend some time with his mother, who was still living.   While sitting in the doorway one day, with his Mother, he was again confronted with the proposition of reenlisting. He agreed to do so for one year, to serve as guard at Fortress Monroe. He remained there until the close of the War, offering brave and faithful services.

Mr. Grandy is now ninety-five years old, residing at 609 Smith Street, Norfolk, Virginia. He is still able to attend the various conventions of Civil War Veterans. He can read, write, and has a fair knowledge of the Bible. His main interest is the organization of Negroes into strong groups. He enjoys talking about religion and is quite an interesting and intelligent person to talk with.

Ex-Slaves Narratives from Mississippi

Adora Rienshaw

"I wuz borned at Beulah, down hyar whar Garner am now, an' my parents wuz Cameron an' Sally Perry. When I wuz a month old we moved ter Raleigh.

"We wuz called 'Ole Issues', case we wuz mixed wid de whites. My pappy wuz borned free, case his mammy wuz a white 'oman an' his pappy wuz a coal-black nigger man. Hit happened in Mississippi, do' I doan know her name 'cept dat she wuz a Perry.

"She wuz de wife of grandfather's marster an' dey said dat he wuz mean ter her. Grandfather wuz her coach-man an' he often seed her cry, an' he'd talk ter her an' try ter comfort her in her troubles, an' dat's de way dat she come ter fall in love wid him.

"One day, he said, she axed him ter stop de carriage an' come back dar an' talk ter her. When he wuz back dar wid her she starts ter cry an' she puts her purtty gold haid on his shoulder, an' she tells him dat he am her only friend, an' dat her husban' won't eben let her have a chile.

"Hit goes on lak dis till her husban' fin's out dat she am gwine ter have de baby. Dey says dat he beats her awful an' when pappy wuz borned he jist about went crazy. Anyhow pappy wuz bound out till he wuz twenty-one an' den he wuz free, case no person wid ary a drap of white blood can be a slave.

"When he wuz free he comed ter Raleigh an' from de fust I can remember he wuz a blacksmith an' his shop wuz on Wolcot's Corner. Dar wuz jist three of us chilluns, Charlie, Narcissus, an' me an' dat wuz a onusual small family.

"Before de war Judge Bantin's wife teached us niggers on de sly, an' atter de war wuz over de Yankees started Hayes's school. I ain't had so much schoolin' but I teached de little ones fer seberal years.

"De southern soldiers burned de depot, which wuz between Cabarrus an' Davie Streets den, an' dat wuz ter keep de Yankees from gittin' de supplies. Wheeler's Cavalry wuz de meanest troops what wuz.

"De Yankees ain't got much in Raleigh, case de Confederates has done got it all an' gone. Why fer a long time dar de way we got our salt wuz by boilin' de dirt from de smoke house floor where de meat has hung an' dripped.

Ex-Slaves Narratives from Mississippi

"I'm glad slavery is ober, eben do' I ain't neber
been no slave. But I tell yo' it's bad ter be a 'Ole
Issue'."

Sam T. Stewart

"My name is Sam T. Stewart. I was born in Wake County,
North Carolina Dec. 11, 1853. My father was a slave, A. H.
Stewart, belonging to James Arch Stewart, a slave owner,
whose plantation was in Wake County near what is now the
Harnett County line of Southern Wake. Tiresa was my mother's
name. James Arch Stewart, a preacher, raised my father,
but my mother was raised by Lorenzo Franks, a Quaker in
Wake County. When I was two years old James Arch Stewart
sold my father to speculators, and he was shipped to Mississippi. I was too young to know my father.

"The names of the speculators were--Carter Harrison,
and--, and a man named Roulhac. I never saw my father
again, but I heard from him the second year of the surrender, through his brother and my aunt. My father died
in Mississippi.

"The speculators bought up Negroes as a drover would
buy up mules. They would get them together by 'Negro
drivers', as the white men employed by the speculators
were called. Their names were,------Jim Harris of Raleigh,
and------yes, Dred Thomas, who lived near Holly Springs
in Wake County. Wagon trains carried the rations on the
trip to Mississippi. The drivers would not start until

they had a large drove. Then the slaves were fastened together with chains. The chain was run between them, when
they had been lined up like soldiers in double file. A
small chain was attached to a Negro on the left and one
to the Negro on the right and fastened to the main chain
in the center. Billy Askew was another speculator. He
lived on the corner of Salisbury and Carbarrus Street in
Raleigh. Sometimes as many as thirty slaves were carried
in a drove. They walked to Mississippi.

"My brothers and sisters are dead. Down on the plantations our houses were built of po__s daubed with mud,
with a rived board (split board). I had good beds, good
clothes, and plenty to eat. We made it and we ate it.
When a slave owner treated his slaves unusually good some
other slave owner would tell him that he was raising slaves
who would rise against him. Lorenzo Franks, who owned
me and my mother, was a Quaker. He treated his slaves
unusually well. He would not sell any of them. His
brother was an Iron Side Baptist preacher, and he would
tell his brother he was raising slaves who would rise
against him. Franks owned seventeen slaves. I don't
know how many Stewart owned.

"I did farm work in slavery time. I earned no
money except what we made on patches. These patches were
given to my mother by my master. We caught birds and

game, sent it to town, and sold it for money. We caught
birds and partridges in traps. Our master would bring them
to town, sell them for us, and give us the money. We had
a lot of possums and other game to eat. We got our food
out of the big garden planted for the whole shebang. My
master overseered his plantation.

"We didn't think much of the poor white man. He was
down on us. He was driven to it, by the rich slave owner.
The rich slave owner wouldn' let his Negroes sociate with
poor white folks. Some of the slave owners, when a poor
white man's land joined theirs and they wanted his place
would have their Negroes steal things and carry them to
the poor white man, and sell them to him. Then the slave
owner, knowing where the stuff was, (Of course the slave
had to do what his master told him.) would go and find
his things at the poor white man's house. Then he would
claim it, and take out a writ for him, but he would give
him a chance. He would tell him to sell out to him, and
leave, or take the consequences. That's the way some of
the slave owners got such large tracks of lands.

"The free Negro was a child by a white man and a
colored woman, or a white woman and a Negro slave. A
child by a white man and a Negro woman was set free when
the man got ready. Sometimes he gave the free Negro slaves.
Oscar Austin, an issue, was set free and given slaves by
his master and daddy. Old man Oscar Austin lived by the

depot in Raleigh. He is dead now.

"When a child by a Negro man slave and a white
woman arrived he could not be made a slave, but he was
bound out until he was 21 years old. The man, who ever
wanted him, had him bound to him by the courts and was his
gardeen until he was 21 years old. He could not be made
a slave if he was born of a free woman. There were jails
for slaves called dungeons; the windows were small.
Slaves were put into jail for misdemeanors until court
was held, but a white man could not be kept there over
30 days without giving bond. Whites and slaves were
kept in the same jail house, but in separate rooms.

"They never taught me to read and write; and most
slaves who got any reading and writing certainly stole
it. There were rules against slaves having books. If
the patterollers caught us with books they would whip us.
There were whipping posts on the plantation but patterollers tied Negroes across fences to whip them. There
was no church on the plantation. We had prayer meetings
in the cabins. We had big times at corn shuckings and
dances. We all had plenty of apple and peach brandy
but very few got drunk. I never saw a nigger drunk
until after the surrender. We went to the white folks'
church. We were partitioned off in the church.

Ex-Slaves Narratives from Mississippi

"The patterollers visited our house every Saturday
night, generally. We set traps to catch the patterollers.
The patterollers were poor white men. We stretched
grape vines across the roads, then we would run from them.
They would follow, and get knocked off their horses. I
knew many of the patterollers. They are mostly dead.
Their children, who are living now in Wake County and
Raleigh, are my best friends, and I will therefore not
tell who they were. I was caught by the patterollers in
Raleigh.

"I would have been whipped to pieces if it hadn't
been for a white boy about my age by the name of Thomas
Wilson. He told them I was his nigger, and they let me
go. We had brought a load of lightwood splints in bundles
to town on a steer cart. This was near the close of the
war. We had sold out one load of splints and had been
paid for them in Confederate money. We had several bills.
We went into a bar and bought a drink, each paying one
dollar a drink, or two dollars for two small drinks.
The bar was in the house where the Globe Clothing Store
is now located on the corner of Wilmington and Exchange
Streets. Just as I swallowed my drink a constable grabbed
me by the back of the. neck, and started with me to the
guard house, where they done their whippin'; Down at the

guard house Nick Denton, the bar tender, told Thomas
Wilson 'Go, tell the constable that is your nigger'.
Thomas came running up crying, and told the constable
I was his nigger. The constable told him to take me and
carry me on home or he would whip both of us. We then
hitched our ox to the cart and went home.

"When I was a child I played marbles, 'Hail over',
and bandy, a game played like golf. In striking the ball
we knocked it at each other. Before we hit the ball we
would cry, 'Shins, I cry', then we would knock the ball
at our playmates. Sometime we used rocks for balls.

"We got Christmas holidays from Christmas to New
Years day. This was also a time when slaves were hired
out or sold. You were often put on the auction block
at Christmas. There was a whipping post, an auction
block, and jail located on Court House Square where the
news stand is now located on Fayetteville Street. There
was a well in the yard.

"We were treated by doctors when sick. We were
given lots of herbs.

"I do not believe in ghosts.

"I did not feel much elated over hearing I was
free, I was afraid of Yankee soldiers. Our mistress
told us we were free. I farmed first year after the

war. We had no horses, the Yankees had taken the horses, and some of us made a crap with grubbing hoes.

"I think Abraham Lincoln was a man who aimed to do good, but a man who never got to it. I cannot say anymore than that his intentions were good, and if he had lived he would have done more good.

Mary Lindsay

My slavery days wasn't like most people tell you about, 'cause I was
give to my young Mistress and sent away to Texas when I was jest a little girl,
and I didn't live on a big plantation a very long time.

I got an old family Bible what say I was born on September 20, in
1846, but I don't know who put de writing in it unless it was my mammy's
mistress. My mammy had de book when she die.

My mammy come out to the Indian country from Mississippi two years
before I was born. She was the slave of a Chickasaw part-breed name Sobe
Love. He was the kinsfolks of Mr. Benjamin Love, and Mr. Henry Love what
bring two big bunches of the Chickasaws out from Mississippi to the Choctaw
country when the Chickasaws sign up de treaty to leave Mississippi, and the
whole Love family settle 'round on the Red River below Fort Washita. There
whar I was born.

My mammy say dey have a terrible hard time again the sickness when
they first come out into that country, because it was low and swampy and all
full of cane brakes, and everybody have the smallpox and the malaria and
fever all the time. Lots of the Chickasaw families nearly died off.

Old Sobe Love marry her off to a slave named William, what belong to
a full-blood Chickasaw man name Chick-a-lathe, and I was one of de children.

De children belong to the owner of the mother, and me and my brother
Franklin, what we called "Bruner", was born under the name of Love and then old
Master Sobe bought my pappy William, and we was all Love slaves then. My
mammy had two more girls, name Hetty and Rena.

My mammy name was Mary, and I was named after her. Old Mistress name was Lottie, and they had a daughter name Mary. Old Master Sobe was powerful rich, and he had about a hundred slaves and four or five big pieces of that bottom land broke out for farms. He had niggers on all the places, but didn't have no overseers, jest hisself and he went around and seen that everybody behave and do they work right.

Old Master Sobe was a mighty big man in the tribe, and so was all his kinfolks, and they went to Fort Washita and to Boggy Depot all the time on business, and leave the Negroes to look after old Mistress and the young daughter. She was almost grown along about that time, when I can first remember about things.

'Cause my name was Mary, and so was my mammy's and my young Mistress' too, Old Master Sobe called me Mary-Ka-Chubbe to show which Mary he was talking about.

Miss Mary have a black woman name Vici what wait on her all the time, and do the carding and spinning and cooking 'round the house, and Vici belong to Miss Mary. I never did go 'round the Big House, but jest stayed in the quarters with my mammy and pappy and helped in the field a little.

Then one day Miss Mary run off with a man add married him, and old Master Sobe nearly went crazy! The man was name Bill Merrick, and he was a poor blacksmith and didn't have two pair of britches to his name, and old Master Sobe said he jest stole Miss Mary 'cause she was rich, and no other reason. 'Cause he was a white man and she was mostly Chickasaw Indian.

Anyways old Master Sobe wouldn't even speak to Mr. Bill, and wouldn't let him set foot on the place. He jest reared and pitched around, and threatened to shoot him if he set eyes on him, and Mr. Bill took Miss Mary and left out for Texas. He set up a blacksmith shop on the big road between Bonham and Honey Grove, and lived there until he died.

Ex-Slaves Narratives from Mississippi

Miss Mary done took Vici along with her, and pretty soon she come back home and stay a while, and old Master Sobe kind of soften up a little bit and give her some money to git started on, and he give her me too.

Dat jest nearly broke my old mammy's and pappy's heart, to have me took away off from them, but they couldn't say nothing and I had to go along with Miss Mary back to Texas. When we git away from the big house I jest cried and cried until I couldn't hardly see, my eyes was so swole up, but Miss Mary said she gwine to be good to me.

I ask her how come Master Sobe didn't give her some of the grown boys and she say she reckon it because he didn't want to help her husband out none, but jest wanted to help her. If he give her a man her husband have him working in the blacksmith shop, she reckon.

Master Bill Merrick was a hard worker, and he was more sober than most the men in them days, and he never tell me to do nothing. He jest let Miss Mary tell me what to do. They have a log house close to the shop, and a little patch of a field at first, but after awhile he git more land, and then Miss Mary tell me and Vici we got to help in the field too.

That sho' was hard living then! I have to git up at three o'clock sometimes so I have time to water the hosses and slop the hags and feed the chickens and milk the cows, and then git back to the house and git the breakfast. That was during the times when Miss Mary was having and nursing her two children, and old Vici had to stay with her all the time. Master Bill never did do none of that kind of work, but he had to be in the shop sometimes until way late in the night, and sometimes before daylight, to shoe peoples hosses and oxen and fix wagons.

Salomon Oliver

John A. Miller owned the finest plantation in Washington County, Mississippi, about 12-mile east of Greenville. I was born on this 20,000-acre plantation November 17, 1859, being one of about four hundred slave children on the place.

About three hundred negro families living in box-type cabins made it seem like a small town. Built in rows, the cabins were kept whitewashed, neat and orderly, for the Master was strict about such things. Several large barns and storage buildings were scattered around the plantation. Also, two cotton gins and two old fashioned presses, operated by horses and mules, made Miller's plantation one of the best equipped in Mississippi.

Master John was quite a character. The big plantation didn't occupy all his time. He owned a bank in Vicksburg and another in New Orleans, and only came to the plantation two or three times a year for a week or two visit.

Things happened around there mighty quick when the Master showed up. If the slaves were not being treated right - out go the white overseer. Fired! The Master was a good man and tried to hire good boss men. Master John was bad after the slave women. A yellow child show up every once in a while. Those kind always got special privileges because the Master said he didn't want his children whipped like the rest of them slaves.

My own Mammy, Mary, was the Master's own daughter! She married Salomon Oliver (who took the name of Oliver after the War), and the Master told all the slave drivers to leave her alone and not whip her. This made the overseers jealous of her and caused trouble. John Santhers was one of the white overseers who treated her bad, and after I was born and got strong enough (I was a weakling for three-four years after birth), to do light chores he would whip me just for the fun of it. It was fun for him but not for me. I hoped to whip him when I grew up. That is the one thing I won't ever forget. He died about the end of the War so that's one thing I won't ever get to do.

My mother was high-tempered and she knew about the Master's orders not to whip her. I guess sometimes she took advantage and tried to do things that maybe wasn't right. But it did her no good and one of the white men flogged her to death. She died with scars on her back!

Father use to preach to the slaves when a crowd of them could slip off into the woods. I don't remember much about the religious things, only just what Daddy told me when I was older. He was caught several times slipping off to the woods and because he was the preacher I guess they layed on the lash a little harder trying to make him give up preaching.

Ration day was Saturday. Each person was given a peck of corn meal, four pounds of wheat flour, four pounds of pork meat, quart of molasses, one pound of sugar, the same of coffee and a plug of tobacco. Potatoes and vegetables came from the family garden and each slave family was required to cultivate a separate garden.

During the Civil War a battle was fought near the Miller plantation. The Yankees under General Grant came through the country. They burned 2,000 bales of Miller cotton. When the Yankee wagons crossed Bayou Creek the bridge gave way and quite a number of soldiers and horses were seriously injured.

For many years after the War folks would find bullets in the ground. Some of the bullets were 'twins' fastened together with a chain.

Master Miller settled my father upon a piece of land after the War and we stayed on it several years, doing well.

I moved to Muskogee in 1902, coming on to Tulsa in 1907, the same year Oklahoma was made a state. My six wives are all dead, - Liza, Lizzie, Ellen,

Ex-Slaves Narratives from Mississippi

Lula, Elizabeth and Henrietta. Six children, too. George, Anna, Salomon, Nelson, Garfield, Cosmos - all good children. They remember the Tulsa riot and don't aim ever to come back to Oklahoma.

When the riot started in 1922 (I think it was), I had a place on the corner of Pine and Owasso Streets. Two hundred of my people gathered at my place, because I was so well known everybody figured we wouldn't be molested. I was wrong. Two of my horses was shot and killed. Two of my boys, Salomon and Nelson, was wounded, one in the hip, the other in the shoulder. They wasn't bad and got well alright. Some of my people wasn't so lucky. The dead wagon hauled them away!

White men came into the negro district and gathered up the homeless. The houses were most all burned. No place to go except to the camps where armed whites kept everybody quiet. They took my clothes and all my money - $298.00 - and the police couldn't do nothing about my loss when I reported it to them.

That was a terrible time, but we people are better off today that any time during the days of slavery. We have some privileges and they are worth more than all the money in the world!

Ex-Slaves Narratives from Mississippi

Robert T. Grinstead Oklahoma City, Okla.

I was born in Lawrence County, Mississippi, February 17, 1857. My
father's name is Elias Grinstead, a German, and my mother's name is Ann Green-
stead after that of her master. I am a son by my mother and her Master. I
have four other half brother: William (Bill) oldest, Albert, Silas, and John.

I was only eight years of age at freedom and for that reason I was
too young to work and on account of being the son of my Master's I received
no hard treatment and did little or no work. Yet, I wore the same clothing
as did the rest of the slaves: a shirt of lowell for summer and shirt and
trousers for winter and no shoes. I could walk through a briar patch in my
bare feet without sticking one in the bottom of my feet as they were so hard
and resistant.

I was the only child of my Master as he had no wife. When the War
broke out he went to the War and left the plantation in charge of his overseer and his two sisters. As the overseers were hard for them to get along
with they were oftener without an overseer as with one, and therefore they
used one of the Negroes as overseer for the most of the time.

Across the river was another large plantation and slave owner by the
name of Master Wilson. We called him Master too, for he was a close friend
and neighbor to our Mistresses. There was one Negro man slave who decided to
not work after Master went to the War and the white overseer was fired and
the Negro overseer was acting as overseer, so my Mistress gave him a note to
take across the river to Master Wilson. The note was an order to whip this
Negro and as he couldn't read he didn't know what the note contained until
after Master Wilson read it and gave orders to his men to tie him for his whipping. After this, the whipping was so severe that they never had any more

trouble in making this Negro slave work and they never had to send him back
again to Master Wilson to be whipped. The fun part of this above incidence
was the Negro carried his own note and went alone to be whipped and didn't
know it 'til the lashes was being put on him.

My Master's plantation was about 2 miles long and 1½ mile wide and he
owned between 30 or 40 slaves. The Negro overseer would wake up the slaves and
have them in the field before they could see how to work each morning and as
they would go to work so soon their breakfast was carried to the field to them.
One morning the breakfast was taken to the field and the slaves were hoeing
cotton and among them was a lad about 15 years of ago who could not hoe as fast
as the older slaves and the breakfast was sat at the end of the rows and as
they would hoe out to the end they would eat, and if you would be late hoeing
to the end the first to ge to the end would began eating and eat everything.
So, this 15 year old lad in order to get out to eat before everything was gone
did not hoe his row good and the overseer, who was white at this time, whipped
him so severely that he could not eat nor work that day.

The Negroes went to church with the white people and joined their
church. The church was Baptist in denomination, and they built a pen in the
church in which the Negroes sat, and when they would take sacrament the
Negroes would be served after the whites were through and one of the Negro
group would pass it around to the others within the pen.

As there were no dances held on the plantation the Negroes would oftimes
slip off and go at nights to a nearby dance or peanut parching or rice suppers
at nights after work. Some of the slaves would be allowed to make for themselves rice patches which they would gather and save for the dances. To pre-
pare this rice for cooking after harvested they would burn a trough into a
log, they called mortar and with a large wooden mallet they called pessel, and
which they would pound upon the rice until hulled and ready for cooking. This

rice would be boiled with just salt and water and eaten as a great feast with delight.

During slavery some of the Negro slaves would kill snakes and skin them and wear these snake skins to prevent being voodooed they said. When some of the slaves would take sick and the home remedies would fail to cure them our Mistress would allow one of the Negro men slaves to go to the white doctor and get some medicine for the patient. The doctor would ask questions as to the actions of the patient and from said description would send medicine without ever going to see the patient and his medicine would always cure the patient of his disease if consulted in time.

After the news came that brought our freedom a white union officer with 20 trained Negro soldiers visited the plantations and saw that the Negroes received their freedom. He would put on a demonstration with his Negro soldiers by having them line up and then at a command they would all rush forward and stand their guns up together on the stock end without a one falling and get back into line and upon another command they would rush forward and each get his gun again without allowing one to fall and again reline up.

When I was large enough to pay attention to my color and to that of the other slaves I wondered to myself why I was not black like the rest of the slaves and concluded to myself that I would when I got grown like they were as I knew not then that I was the son of my Master.

During the War and as the men and our Master all went to the War the Negroes or a Negro would have to go to the Mistress' homes each morning and start fires and never, did I ever hear of a rape case under such close conditions as Negroes going into the bed rooms each morning of the white mistress to start fires.

My first wife was name Tracy Smith. As I had been free for over

12 years. We had ordinary marriage ceremony. I have 11 grown children, 15 or 20 grandchildren and 3 great grandchildren.

I think Abraham Lincoln was a fine old gentlemen and as to Jeff Davis I don't think he was what he should have been, and as to Booker T. Washington I think his idea of educating or training Negroes as servants to serve the white race appealed more to the white race than the Negroes.

My viewpoint as to slavery is that it was as much detrimental to the white race as it was to the Negroes, as one elevated ones minds toohighly, and the other degraded ones mind toolowly.

Ex-Slaves Narratives from Aberdeen, Mississippi

<u>George Greene</u>

Birth and Age

"I don't know when I was born. I don't know exactly, but I was born in
slavery time before the War began. I was big enough to wait on the table
when they was fighting. I remember when they was setting the Negroes free.
I was born in Aberdeen, Mississippi, in Monroe County. Seven miles from the
town of Aberdeen, out on the prairies, that is where I was born.

"I figure out my age by the white woman that raised me. She sent me my
age. When they was working the roads, my road boss, I told him I was forty-
five years old and he didn't believe it. So I sent to the white woman that
raised me from a month-old child. When I left her, I'd done got grown. Her
name was Narcissus Stephenson; she had all our ages and she sent mine to me.

"She may be dead now. I could've stayed right there if she isn't dead,
because she never did want me to come away. Right out in Arkansas, I come,—
to my sorrow. Well, I done right well till I got crippled. Got hit by an
automobile. That's what I'm doin' here now.

Parents and Relatives

"My father's name was Nathan Greene. I reckon he went by that name,
I can't swear to it. I wasn't with him when he died. I was up in Mississippi on the Mississippi River and didn't get the news in time to get
there till after he was dead. He was an old soldier. When the Yankees got
down in Mississippi, they grabbed up every nigger that was able to fight.

If I'd get his furlough papers, I'd a been drawin' pension before I did.
But his brother was with him when he died and he let the dismiss papers get
lost, and nobody got nothin'. Don't draw nothin' from it at all. Couldn't
find the papers when I was down there.

"I don't know whether my father used his master's name or his father's
name. His father's name was Jerry Greene, and his master's name was Henry
Bibb. I don't know which name he went by, but I call myself Greene because
his father's name was Jerry Greene. No Bibb owned him at first. Jerry
Greene was born in North, Alabama in Morgan County. That's where he was
born. Bibb bought him and brought him down to Mississippi where I was born.
Lord! Old Man Bibb owned a lot of 'em, too. My father and grandfather were
both colored but my grandfather was an old yellow man. You know, he had to
take his color after his papa. I don't know my great-grandfather's name.
They can't tell nothin' 'bout that in them days. His papa, my grandfather's
papa, I can't tell for sure whether he was white or black.

"My mother's name was Adeline Greene. Grandpa's wife's name was Louisa.
She was one of these kinder mixed with Indian. She lived to see a many a
year before she died. She lived to be a hundred and fifteen years of age
before she died. I knowed Grandma Louisa. Up until I was a man grown. She
was about my color with long straight hair and black (hair). Old Lady Bibb
was her mistress. She died way after freedom.

"I don't know mama's age. I was here in Arkansas when she died.
Didn't know she was dead until a month after she was buried. She died in
Mississippi. Grandma, mama, and all of them died in Mississippi.

"My grandma on my mother's side was named--I can't remember her name,
but I knowed her. I can't remember what the old man's name was neither. It's
been so long it just went from my memory. They never told me much neither.

Ex-Slaves Narratives from Aberdeen, Mississippi

Folks didn't talk much to children in those days. I wouldn't hardly have
thought of it now anyway.

House and Furniture

"A old log house was what I was born in,---when I come out from Mississippi that old house was still standing. Aw, they put up houses them
days. It had one room. Didn't have but one room,---one window, one door,---
didn't have but one door to go in and out. I remember that well. Didn't
have no whole parcel of doors to go in and out. Plank floors. I wasn't
born on the dirt! I was born on planks. Our house was up off the ground.
We had a board roof. We used four foot boards. Timber was plentiful then
where they could make boards easy. Boards was cheap. There wasn't no such
things as shingles. Didn't have no shingle factories.

"We didn't have nothing but an old wooden bed. It wasn't bought. It
was made. Made it at home. Carpenter made it. Making wooden beds was
perfect then. They'd break down every two or three years. They lasted.
There was boards holding then. Wasn't no slats nor nothing. Nail them
boards to the post and to the sides of the house, and that was the end of it
with some people. We had a corded bed. Put them ropes through the sides
and corded them up there as tight as Dick's hatband--and they stayed. They
made their own boards, and made their own ropes, and corded them together,
and they stayed. Chairs! Shucks! They just took boxes. They made chairs
too--took shucks and put bottoms in them. Them chairs lasted. Them shucks
go way, they'd put more there. Wish I had one of them chairs now. We made
a box and put our rations in it. Them days they made what they called
cupboards. They made anything they wanted to. When they got free, they'd
buy dishes. When they got free, boxes and cupboards went out of style.

Ex-Slaves Narratives from Aberdeen, Mississippi

They bought safes. There wasn't no other furniture. We used tin pans for dishes in slavery time. When we got free, we bought plates.

"When them pans fell they didn't break. They even as much as made their own trays to make bread in. They would take a cypress tree and dig it out and them scoundrels lasted too. Don't see nothin' like that now. Tin pan is big enough to make up bread in now. In them days they made anything. Water buckets,—they did buy them. Old master would give 'em a pass to go get 'em. Anything they wanted, he would give 'em if he thought it necessary. Old master would get 'em all the buckets. He was good and he would buy what you would ask him for. They made milk buckets. They made 'em just like they make 'em now.

Work of Family in Slave Time

"My people were all field hands. My master had a great big farm—three or four hundred acres. I waited table when I was a little chap and I learned to plow before the War was over.

Good Master

"Old Man Bibb was as good and clever a man as ever you knowed. That overseer down there, if he whipped a man Old Man Bibbs would say, 'Here's your money. Don't want you beating up my niggers so they can't work. I don't need you.' He'd tell 'im quick he don't need him and he can git. That's the kind of man he was. Wouldn't let you be mobbed up. He was a good christian man. I'll give that to him. In the time of the War when they was freeing slaves and I was a little old eight-year-old kid, there was a little old Dutchman, a Tennessee man, he came out in the country to get feed. Out there in Alabama.

Ex-Slaves Narratives from Aberdeen, Mississippi

"I was in Alabama then. The white woman that raised me had taken me
there. She had done married again and left me with mama awhile. While I
was little, that was. When I was about seven, she came and got me again and
carried me down in Alabama and raised me with her children. That white
woman never called me nothin' but baby as long as she lived. You know she
cared for me just like I was one of her's. When a person raise a child from
a month old she can't help from loving it.

"This Dutchman came and asked me where my parents was and I told him
they was in Mississippi. He slipped me away from my folks and carried me to
Decatur and they got cut off there. He was a Yankee soldier, and old
Forrest's army caught 'em and captured me and then carried me first nearly
to Nashville. They got in three miles of the town and couldn't get no
closer. They ran us so we never got no res' till we got to Booneville,
Mississippi. Then I sent word to Bibb and my uncle came up and got me. Him
and Billie Bibb, my young master. Billie Bibb was a soldier too. He was
home on a furlough. I was glad to see him because I tell you in the army
there was suffering. But I'll tell you I'll give them credit, those Tennessee men took care of me just as though I was their own. I was in a two
mule wagon. I drove it. I was big enough to drive. The ambulance man
stopped in Nashville to see his folks and got a furlough and went on home.

Work

"I learned how to work—work in the field. Wasn't nothing but field
work. I learned how to hoe first. But in Alabama I learned how to plow. I
didn't want to be no hoe man; I wanted to plow. When I went back to Mississippi, they put me on the plow. I was just eight years old when I learned
to plow.

Ex-Slaves Narratives from Aberdeen, Mississippi

Share cropping

"Right after freedom, I just kept on plowing. We share cropped. My mama and I would take a crop. She'd work. We'd all work like the devil until I got a job and went to town. She was willing to let me go. That was when I married too.

How Freedom Came

"All I know about freedom was Old Man Henry Bibb come out and told us we was free. That is how I came to know it. He came out there on the farm and said, 'Well, you all free as I am. You can stay here if you want to or you can go somewhere else.' We stayed. Mama stayed there on the farm plumb till she come to town. I don't know how many years. I was there in town and so she came onto town later. Moved in with the people she was with. They gave up their place. I was nineteen years old when I left the country. My mother gave me her consent,--to marry then, too. She came to town a few years later.

"The slaves weren't given nothin' after they was freed. Nothing but what they worked for. They got to be share croppers.

Ku Klux Klan

"The Ku Klux never bothered me but they sure bothered others. Way yonder in Mississippi directly after the surrender, they'd hated it so bad they killed up many of them. They caught white men there and whipped them and killed them. They killed many a nigger. They caught a white man there and whipped him and he went on up to Washington, D. C. and came back with a train load of soldiers. They came right down there in the south end of our town and they carried them Ku Kluxers away by train loads full. They cleaned out the east side of the river. The Ku Klux had been stringing up niggers

every which way. 'Twasn't nothin' to find a nigger swinging up in the woods.
But those soldiers come from Washington City. If they didn't clean 'em up,
I'll hush.

"I don't know what become of 'em. They never did come back to
Aberdeen.

Occupations Followed and Life
Since Freedom

"I ain't worked a lick in four or five years. If I lived to see August
tenth, I will be eighty-six years old. I used to follow railroading or saw
milling or farming. That is what I followed when I was able to work. The
last work I did was farming, working by the day—a dollar and a half a day.
And they cut it down and cut me down. Now they ain't giving nothing. If a
man gets six bits a day he doing good. Harder times in Arkansas now than I
have ever seen before. If a man is able to take care of his family now, he
is doing well. They don't give niggers nothing now.

"The only way I live is I get a little pension. They give me eight
dollars a month and commodities. That is all I live on now. That keeps me
up, thank God. I have been getting the pension about ever since they
started. I reckon it is about two years. I have been receiving it every
month. It ain't failed yet. They been taking care of me pretty well ever
since they started. First start it wasn't nothin' but rations. They give
me groceries enough to las' me every month. I had a wife then.

"I have been a _widow_ now four years. Four years I've been a _widow_.
But there ain't nothin' like a man staying in his own house. I have made
out now for four years. Right there cooking and washing for George! I
didn't have nothing else to do. Fellow can't tell what day the Lord will
say, 'Stop', but as long as I am this way, I'll keep at it.

Ex-Slaves Narratives from Aberdeen, Mississippi

"This soreness in my leg keeps me in bad shape. I came here to get my leg fixed. It gets so I can't walk without a stick. I don't like to stay with other folks. They're sinners and they use me sorta sinful--speak any sort of language. But they sure 'nough treats me nice.

"I got my leg hurt last December. Car ran into me at Wrightsville, and knocked me down and threw me far as from here to that thing (about fifteen feet). After they flung me down, I was flat on my back a long while. I couldn't move. When a fellow gets old and then gets crippled up, it's hard. But I'm gettin' 'long pretty well now, 'cept that this leg ain't strong."

Express Your Thoughts

Express Your Thoughts

Express Your Thoughts

"You can triumph and come to skill. You can be great if you only will. You are well equipped for what fight you choose. You have legs and arms and a brain to use. And the man who has risen great deeds to do; began his life with no more than YOU."

- Edgar A. Guest

Express Your Thoughts

"Truth is within; never stop believing."

- Dr. Roderick Van Daniel

Express Your Thoughts

"Truth in the Lord with all thine heart and lean not unto thine own understanding."

- Proverbs 3:5

Express Your Thoughts

"One important key to success is self confidence. An important key to self-confidence is preparation."

   – Arthur Ashe

Express Your Thoughts

"People are not remembered by how few times they failed, but by how often
they succeed. Every wrong step can be another step forward."

- Thomas Edison

Express Your Thoughts

"Some men have thousands of reasons why they cannot do what they want to do when all they really need is one reason why they can."

- Willis Whitney

Express Your Thoughts

"But even in the inevitable moments when all seems hopeless, men know that without hope they cannot really live, and in agonizing desperation they cry for the bread of hope."

- Dr. Martin Luther King, Jr.

Express Your Thoughts

"This I recall to my mind, therefore have I hope. It is of the Lord's mercies that we are not consumed, because his compassions fail not. They are new every morning: great is thy faithfulness. The Lord is my portion, saith my soul; therefore will I hope in him. The Lord is good unto them that wait for him, to the soul that seeketh him. It is good that a man should both hope and quietly wait for the salvation of the Lord."

Lamentations 3:21-26

Express Your Thoughts

"There are good men and bad men of all nationalities, creeds and color; and
if this world of ours is ever to become what we hope someday it may become, it
must be by the general recognition that the man' s heart and soul, the man' s
worth and actions, determine his standing."

- President Theodore Roosevelt

Express Your Thoughts

"Keep your mind focus on your goals. Do not let the distractions of life hold you back from accomplishing your task from positive to negative. Live long and strong. Simply Believe."

    - Dr. Roderick Van Daniel

Express Your Thoughts

"Never stop giving your best even when the world tells you that your best is not good enough. Simply Believe."

  - Dr. Roderick Van Daniel

"And we know that all things work together for good to them that love God, to them who are the called according to His purpose."

- Romans 8:28

Express Your Thoughts

"Believe in your aspirations in life. Believe in yourself. Have a strategy. Make it become your reality. Simply Believe."

- Dr. Roderick Van Daniel

Express Your Thoughts

"Those who hope in the Lord will renew their strength. They will soar on wings like eagles; they will run and not grow weary, they will walk and not be faint."

  - Isaiah 40:31

Express Your Thoughts

"But hope that is seen is no hope at all. Who hopes for what he already have, we wait for it patiently. In the same way, the Spirit helps us in our weakness. We do not know what we ought to pray for, but the Spirit himself intercedes for us with groans that words cannot express. And he who searches our hearts knows the mind of the Spirit."

- Romans 8:24-27

Express Your Thoughts

"Now faith is being sure of what we hope for and certain of what we do not see. And without faith it is impossible to please God, because anyone who comes to him must believe that he exists and that he rewards those who earnestly seek him."

— Hebrews 11:1,6

Conclusion

Conclusion

It is hard to understand why African Americans are imprisoned at higher rates than other racial class in the United States of America without having knowledge of what the Black Codes were. These discriminatory and restrictive laws criminalized negroes after slavery and set the stage for the Jim Crow laws.

Also, the Black Codes is a directly link to the present day prison systems of America. Given this knowledge, I hope this book gives you a better understanding of the Black Codes and their relationship to the 13th Amendment providing a historical background for racial profiling, police brutality, and uneven criminal sentencing toward African Americans.

References

References

Gibson, Arrell M.
1971   The Chickasaws. University of Oklahoma Press, Norman, Oklahoma.

Gilleylan, H. S.
1908-1912   Manuscript Account Book. Evans Memorial Library, Aberdeen, Mississippi.

1916   Manuscript Account Book, Prairie Plantation Company. Evans Memorial Library, Aberdeen, Mississippi.

1917   Manuscript Account Book, Prairie Plantation Company. Evans Memorial Library, Aberdeen, Mississippi.

1918   Manuscript Account Book, Prairie Plantation Company. Evans Memorial Library, Aberdeen, Mississippi.

Kern, John R., Ira Berlin, C. Stephan Demeter, Steven F. Miller and Judith D. Tordoff
1982a   Phase I Interdisciplinary Investigations at Sharpley's Bottom Historic Sites, Tombigbee River Multiresource District, Alabama and Mississippi. Interim report. Commonwealth Associates, Inc., Jackson, Michigan, submitted to National Park Service.

Kern, John R., Ira Berlin, Steven F. Miller, Joseph P. Reidy and Leslie S. Rowland
1982b   Sharpley's Bottom Historic Sites: Phase II Historical Investigations Tombigbee River Multiresource District, Alabama and Mississippi. Final report. Commonwealth Associates, Inc., Jackson, Michigan, submitted to National Park Service.

Monroe County Deed Book
1836-1968   Manuscript Volumes. Monroe County Chancery Court, Aberdeen, Mississippi.

Monroe County Deeds of Trust
1875   Manuscript Volume. Monroe County Chancery Court, Aberdeen, Mississippi.

Sharpley, Louisa A. v. William B. Sharpley
1865   Cause 353. Monroe County Chancery Court, Aberdeen, Mississippi.

Sharpley, Maggie and Letha Sharpley v. John F. Plant
1897-1901   Cause 3093. Monroe County Chancery Court, Aberdeen, Mississippi.

Sharpley, Wallace et al. v. B. C. Sims et al.
1889-1890   Causes 2513-2516. Monroe County Chancery Court, Aberdeen, Mississippi.

References

U. S. Bureau of the Census
1872   The Statistics of the Population of the United States. Ninth Census. Government Printing Office, Washington.

U. S. Census Manuscripts, Agriculture
1850   Seventh Census, Manuscript Schedule, Monroe County, Mississippi. Microfilm, Southern Historical Collection, University of North Carolina, Chapel Hill.

1860   Eighth Census, Manuscript Schedule, Monroe County, Mississippi. Microfilm, Southern Historical Collection, University of North Carolina, Chapel Hill.

U. S. Census Manuscripts, Population
1840   Sixth Census, Manuscript Schedule, Mecklenburg County, North Carolina. Microfilm, National Archives, Washington, D.C.

1850   Seventh Census, Manuscript Schedule, Monroe County, Mississippi. Microfilm, National Archives, Washington, D.C.

1860   Eighth Census, Manuscript Schedule, Monroe County, Mississippi. Microfilm, National Archives, Washington, D.C.

1870   Ninth Census, Manuscript Schedule, Monroe County, Mississippi. Microfilm, National Archives, Washington, D.C.

U. S. Census Manuscripts, Slave Population
1850   Seventh Census, Manuscript Schedule, Monroe County, Mississippi. Microfilm, National Archives, Washington, D.C.

1860   Eighth Census, Manuscript Schedule, Monroe County, Mississippi. Microfilm, National Archives, Washington, D.C.

Whitfield, Theodore Marshall
1948   Whitfield, Bryan, Smith and Related Families. n.p.

Whitfield-Wooten Papers
1829-1858 Manuscript Letters and Documents. Southern Historical Collection, University of North Carolina, Chapel Hill.

Author

Dr. Roderick Van Daniel was born in Aberdeen, Mississippi. He presently lives in the Washington D.C. area. If you need for me to speak or order books; contact me. Thanks for your time. I appreciate you all.

Contact:

      roddaniel205@gmail.com

      Instagram: @drroderickvandaniel

"Knowledge is important. Growth is starts from within you. Fairness for all is in your heart and mind. Never stop striving to help others."

    -Dr. Roderick Van Daniel